GRACE
CHOICES

GRACE
CHOICES

WALKING IN STEP WITH THE
GOD OF GRACE

JEFF LUCAS

Authentic

First published 2004 by Spring Harvest Publishing Division
and Authentic Media,
9 Holdom Avenue, Bletchley, Milton Keynes, Bucks, MK1 1QR UK
and PO Box 1047, Waynesboro, GA 30830-2047, USA
www.authenticmedia.co.uk

British Library Cataloguing in Publication Data
A catalogue record for this book is available from the British
Library

ISBN 1-85078-554-6

Cover design by David Lund
Print Management by Adare Carwin
Printed and Bound in Denmark by Nørhaven Paperback

Hazel
Grace shines through you

And to the wonderful family that is
Timberline Church

With much love and appreciation

Jeff Lucas' latest is a treasure trove of hope, an intelligent, well-written, passionate and of course humourous exploration of the crucial topic of grace – get one for yourself and at least one to give away.
Graham Kendrick

Jeff Lucas is one of the most skilled and effective communicators of Christian truth on either side of the Atlantic. He has the wit of a Ben Elton, the 'common touch' of a Bob Geldof and, just when you need it, the illuminating insight of a contemporary Oswald Chambers. In recent years, Jeff's journey of faith has involved a deep and detailed exploration of the theme of grace. This excellent book is a basket for the fruits of that exploration - ripe, flavourful and ready to eat.
Gerard Kelly, poet, author, speaker and Co-Director of the Bless Network

Vintage Jeff…one of the most relevant books I have read in a long time. Fresh and funny, he manages to shed light on the most essential subject of them all: grace.
R. T. Kendall, author and former Minister of Westminster Chapel

This book is practical theology which earths heaven's grace into everyday experience. Jeff is at his best here untangling religious entrapments and challenging ordinary people to make grace choices. Condemning thoughts scattered as I read, laughed and chose to pick up the phone to congratulate him.
Stuart Bell, Senior Minister of New Life Christian Fellowship, Lincoln

Three words sprang into my heart as I read this book: refreshing, relevant and real. Refreshing in Jeff Lucas' easy witty and poignant style, relevant in the caricatures being about me (maybe you) but it is the realism that shouted loudest. How easy to get caught up in the routine of Christian living and lose the reality of Jesus Christ living his life in us as radically as he lived it in his own body two thousand years ago.
Charles Price, Pastor, The Peoples Church, Toronto, Canada

What we think about, when we think about God, is the most important thing about us. This book, so utterly readable, may change those thoughts forever.
Gerald Coates, Leader Pioneer Network, speaker, author and broadcaster

If you thought *Amazing Grace* was just a catchy lyric this book will put you right. Read it and discover how grace is not just amazing but also contagious. And the world needs an epidemic.
Ian Coffey, Senior Minister, Mutley Baptist Church, Plymouth

This book might just stop the traffic long enough to amaze us all with the grace of God once again. Jeff Lucas is someone I've laughed with, learned from and listened to (carefully) over a number of years. Grace is what he does, what he says, who he is. In this brilliant, profound and searching new book one of the most gifted Bible teachers of our time shares his very life-message. It is humorous and honest, easy-to-read yet hard-to-hold, a familiar theme and yet a fresh and timely exposition to change, challenge and re-charge your life with joy.

Pete Greig, writer and founder of 24-7 Prayer

For each of us life's choice is simply this – to journey with, and in constant pursuit of, the God of grace or to settle for the bitter and biting chill of the cold lands of ungrace. That's why I wholeheartedly recommend *Grace Choices*. Jeff Lucas is my trusted friend; he's honest, thoughtful, thought-provoking and very funny, but most importantly he loves God – all of which mean that this book is a wonderful travel guide for the adventurous.

Steve Chalke MBE, Founder Oasis Trust and Faithworks

Jeff Lucas is an absolute gift to the Church and as far as I'm concerned he never fails to come up with the goods. Once again he's written a brilliant, witty and challenging book.

Andy Hawthorne, Director of The Message Trust

Just now and then you read a book you choose to read all the way through. *Grace Choices* is just that book. Jeff Lucas writes with real connection to our everyday lives and does it with such ease. He makes us laugh and cry whilst learning about things that really matter. *Grace Choices* opens our eyes to see God's grace and in multicolour and with deeper clarity. But more than that; when finished, this book leaves us making radical grace choices.

Ruth Dearnley, Spring Harvest Leadership Team

If you are tired of Christianity and you just want to follow Jesus read this book.

Adrian Plass, author and international speaker

Grace is the jewel we possessed all along but had seemingly mislaid. Jeff Lucas helps us find it, polish it, treasure it.

Rob Parsons, Executive Director, Care for the Family

CONTENTS

INTRODUCTION

A stricken deer

Book signing sessions are a nightmare for most writers. You park yourself behind a table in the strategic epicentre of a bookshop, and sit in the shadow of what seems like a skyscraper of books – books *you've* written, the towering pile of paper a sobering monument to the fact that they are, as yet, unsold.

Pen in hand, you wait, hopeful, praying that some kindly browser will take pity on you and (a) help reduce the stack that eclipses you and (b) ask you to sign the book they buy. Not fun, particularly when they pick up the aforementioned tome, take ten minutes to scan it, then sniff, slap it back down on top of the undiminished pile and walk away.

As book signings go, however, this one was a real treat. It was at Spring Harvest 2002: a comforting line of buyers snaked back quite a way in the bookshop, and I was enjoying the chatter that comes easily when people are on holiday and feeling relaxed: this was fun.

Then a pale, thin-faced lady stepped up to the table. She was nervous, agitated even, and refused to return my smile, preferring to look down. Her fingers fidgeted endlessly with the leather bag strap that dangled limply over her drooping shoulder, and her hurried, half-whispered words made me feel like we were engaging in some kind of furtive conspiracy; which, in a way, we were.

Stealing a quick glance at the line behind her, she thanked me for helping her, through my preaching, to have a moment of laughter the previous evening. Laughter was not something she had experienced for quite a while, she explained, still staring down. A question or two from me revealed that she was actually a prisoner, her clouded eyes her prison garb. She had been taught – probably more by inference than directly – that laughter was a trivial, suspect thing, not appropriate for her. Fun was not really a live word in her vocabulary; it had been trampled in the pursuit of more weighty things. Why, fun was surely silliness, vain and foolish even, to be firmly rejected in favour of more 'profitable' aims. As I listened to her words, I wondered how long she had been so shackled by such sternness. Surely she had laughed, skipped, giggled and had at least moments of being wonderfully dizzy, loud and trite as a child. Somewhere along the way, a cloud had been firmly pulled over her sunshine, and joy had been taught out of her, laughter sent packing; dismissed in the Name of God.

But just last night, she said, the faintest crease in her face hinting at the vaguest dawning of a smile, she had allowed herself the luxury of laughter. She had actually chuckled. She had felt guilty, but good. And then, ever so slowly, a tear overflowed from the corner of her eye and trickled down her cheek to her trembling chin, where it dropped onto her hand. But this was a tear born of relief, mingled with confusion. She had been thrilled and stunned at the notion that God really did like and love her. It was such a wonderful thought, she said. Could it really be true?

> SHE HAD BEEN THRILLED AND STUNNED AT THE NOTION THAT GOD REALLY DID LIKE AND LOVE HER

Of course, she had long believed in the Christian doctrine concerning the God of love. She could probably quote more biblical texts than most to support the idea: it's just that the doctrine had never penetrated beyond the crust of her belief system, had never started to thaw the icy fear that seemed to chill her heart. She would have died a martyr to protect her conviction of divine love, but had never been able to live in it as a reality; her Sunday morning creeds had never brightened her Monday mornings.

Who was the stern governess who had taught her thus? Remarkably, it was her Christian faith. Her church couldn't take all the blame; perhaps she was the victim of a lethal combination of a stern upbringing, too many harsh words pummelling her, and a host of other unknown factors: but her church certainly hadn't helped. She belonged to the kind of congregation that was a well-oiled guilt machine; where people gathered each week to feel bad and feel little else. It was exactly what she didn't need. She was the sad embodiment of psychiatrist Paul Tournier's words: 'The tragic fact is that religion – my own as well as that of all believers – can crush instead of liberate.'[1]

And crushed she was. I guessed that if I asked this bruised lady to use one word to describe how she thought God viewed her, the word 'sinner' would rush immediately to her mind. British clinical psychologist Anne Balfour provides insight into the ungrace that is an epidemic among those who say they believe in such an amazing grace

> In over twenty years of working as a clinical psychologist with Christians, I have discovered that grace is a subject not rooted in people's personal experience, and therefore one that I am passionate about, and end up exploring in my sessions with clients! When I ask people how they think God sees them, they frequently reply that He sees them as 'a sinner', 'dust of the earth', 'a lowly worm', and 'condemned'. It's as if they have a filter to remove words such as 'loved', 'saved by grace', 'a new creation', seeing instead a harsh God of demands and judgements and conditions to be met. When I ask where they got this information from, they quote Bible verses, but leave out vital bits, for example that 'God loved the world and so he gave...

I scrawled an unusually lengthy dedication in the book she was buying: a little ruse to prolong the conversation. I searched urgently for a word, a sentence, a text that might lighten her load. Suddenly, she grabbed the book, and moved quickly away from the signing table: it was as if a meter had clicked in her head – time up. As she disappeared into the crowd of milling shoppers, she glanced back at me, and at the line of people who had

---

[1] Philip Yancey, *What's so amazing about grace?*, (Harper Collins, 1997)

stood patiently behind her. She looked so very guilty. Her facial expression shouted that she was ashamed that she had taken my time: pained that she was the one who had perhaps delayed the queue. Frankly, shame looked terribly natural on her.

I'm not suggesting that she was at all typical. I bump into thousands of Christians in my life of endless travel, and many of them are emotionally rounded and healthy people who know that they are loved by God, and live positive, joy-tinged lives as a result. But I also meet far too many who are wounded, saddened people, for whom the good news has apparently not been that good. And it's not that their sadness stems from a lack of commitment to Jesus – on the contrary, many of them are stalwarts of the faith – but they are committed austere, contained people, hopeful for heaven but emotionally corseted for life on earth. Grace, for them, is an idea but not a transforming kiss. And by this I am not suggesting that every believer needs to have a happy-clappy, laugh-a-second temperament: I am well aware that people experience and express their faith in a great variety of ways. To be quiet and serious is no sin, and there's nothing worse than the Christian cheerleading that sometimes tries to nudge people into being what they are not. The issue here is freedom, not temperament. This dear lady was anything but free.

WHEN I ASK PEOPLE HOW THEY THINK GOD SEES THEM, THEY FREQUENTLY REPLY THAT HE SEES THEM AS 'A SINNER'

She reminded me of something that was said by the poet William Cowper, who wrote some of the most beautiful hymns about grace and redemption, but struggled terribly to accept that *he* could be so loved of God. He was, to use a phrase of his own creation, 'a stricken deer'. One of his poems shows how alienated he felt from the presence and blessing of God, an unwelcome stranger while others were enjoying the banquet: 'Such Jesus is and such His grace, O may He shine on you! And tell Him, when you see His face, I long to see Him too'.

Surprised by joy

Then I met the next person in line.

She was a lady, obviously physically disabled, old before her time. She wheeled herself quickly up to the table, and suddenly the sun came out again. Her body was hunched over in the wheelchair, her arthritic fingers gripping the rubber armrests, whitening her gnarled knuckles, but her eyes were so full of light and life. Her mouth was creased with lovely laughter lines, and she was grinning hugely. In the course of the next few minutes, words of warmth and encouragement would topple easily from her smiling lips: she pressed her head back against the unyielding leather of the wheel chair as she chuckled.

And she had absolutely no such right to be so alive, humanly speaking at least. She was wheelchair-bound because a consistently abusive husband had punched her into a seated position: a posture, barring healing or recovery, which would be hers for the rest of her days. One after another, the doctors had shaken their heads and said that there was no specific root to her disability, no rogue disease to name and perhaps cure: rather, her body had just surrendered to all that day in, day out bruising, and flatly refused to work any more. At least now she had called time on the evil boxing, so she lived alone, but that meant that she was totally reliant on friends from the church to take her shopping, to ferry her to worship services, to be her very lifeline. She had no independence, little money, and terribly narrowed prospects for the future: which made the fact that she was so deliriously content all the more difficult to fathom. Grace had made her into a stunning human being, one totally unshackled by the difficulties of her circumstances. When I asked her how she could dare to be so, those laughter lines creased even deeper as she said but one word: 'Jesus.' With that simple explanation, she taught me that grace is no mere idea, or disembodied principle. Grace is *very* up close and personal, in that it comes in the One who is loaded with – full of – grace and truth. She had not 'learned' grace in the typical workshop/seminar fashion of our day: rather she had *met* grace in meeting Jesus Christ, and in making him her supreme friend, closest ally and loving Lord.

GRACE IS *VERY* UP CLOSE AND PERSONAL

Our few moments of chatter over the book table were over: she got a signed book, and I got a renewed sense of wonder. Jesus really is the light that drives away even the most oppressive darkness.

Later that night, I reflected on my meeting with the two ladies in line. Which of them was I most like, I mused? If truth be told, I am a little like both of them: perhaps most of us are. Like a pinball flipped from one lit post to another, bounding and rebounding in turn, I bounce from moments of great joy, freedom, and friendship with God, to episodes – sometimes seasons – where grace seems more like an irrelevant idea. During these autumnal times, it feels as though God has vacated the universe, and a lingering grey shroud of shame is draped over everything. Hope becomes a dying ember, finally fading to nothing, at least for a while.

Then I wondered: how would it have been if I could have put the two ladies together for a coffee and a couple of hours of unhurried conversation? Would an extended exposure to the sunlight of grace have opened the petals of that fearful heart?

That's the reason for this *Grace choices* book: I want to invite you to take a long, unhurried look at this amazing subject of grace – and, more importantly, at the God of grace himself. Grace is having a heyday – certainly writers far superior to me have penned wonderfully to help us to rediscover the 'charming sound' that is grace. Philip Yancey's *What's so amazing about grace?*[2] and Chuck Swindoll's *The Grace Awakening*[3] are but two of the more contemporary, popular works that have powerfully helped many to freedom.

But I humbly offer the following chapters in the hope that they might help yet more prisoners towards liberation and changed Monday morning lifestyles, rather than just revised Sunday morning belief systems. Certainly a gaze at God and his grace should impact our values, our priorities and every sector of our lives. The chapters that follow provide a challenge to make 'grace choices'. By

[2] Philip Yancey, *What's so amazing about grace?*, (HarperCollins, 1997)

[3] Charles Swindoll, *The Grace Awakening*, (Word Publishing, 1996)

organising the material in this way, I am not suggesting a 'Fifty-nine ways to exude and overflow in grace in one easy and painless lesson' approach. I am well aware that the grace life takes a lifetime to learn, and eternity to celebrate: part of the reason for forever really being eternal is that it will take that long for God to escort us through the gallery of his outrageous kindness, so a quick fix, cheap pathway towards grace is not one that I want to direct us to. And gathering information about him is not enough: grace comes as we allow him to touch, shape, and sometimes (apparently) interfere with our lives.

Yet, as part of the long journey, grace does call us to choose some paths and reject others: grace is intensely practical. Jim Partridge, a respected youth specialist who was much of the creative genius behind the dynamic *Youthwork* conference held in the UK in 2003, expresses well how grace shapes his own sense of everyday identity:

> My generation so desperately needs to hear the message of grace: there is little concept of personal sin out there ... our friends ... look at us and our similar lives and could say on first impressions that Christ has made no material benefit to our lives. Our response is that they spend their lives attaining to wealth, career, and so-called significance – chasing something that may not ever be attainable, and then, if they get it, they will find that significance was never at that location of their ambition in the first place! Yet, in Christ we are secure in our identity ... through grace.

And it's not just about me

I pray that this consideration of grace choices will not be a journey taken only in the name of self: grace is not by any means just about us: it is a planet-shaking force that flows from God's heart. Graceless and godless living is destroying our planet at a pace unparalleled by any ecological threat. Yet unwittingly the world stands on tiptoe waiting for the good news. Our culture is increasingly stained by a million smears of ungrace, as our streets are marred by the incessant spewing of crass language, by ignitions of road rage, by violence and disrespect and day-to-day unkindness. Love is all around, as the makers of last year's hit film *Love Actually* insist, but then so is ungrace. Yet there remains a haunting cry for grace in our culture. The message of relativism – truth is relative to the individual, which ultimately leads to moral anarchy and chaos – fails to satisfy. Cinema, which some believe is the new 'cathedral' of our culture, reflects that angst.

> ⤸ ⤷
>
> THERE REMAINS A HAUNTING CRY FOR GRACE IN OUR CULTURE
>
> ⤸ ⤷

Recent films from the last decade that deal with redemption and grace are *Black Robe* (1991), *Leap of Faith* (1992), *Priest* (1995), *Dead Man Walking* (1995), *A Pure Formality* (1996), *Trainspotting* (1996), *Breaking the Waves* (1996) and *Sling Blade* (1996). *Bruce Almighty*, starring Jim Carrey, echoes the insistent longing for grace, as Carrey's character complains that life is not precisely as he would like it, and so prays 'Oh God, why do you hate me? God is a kid sitting on an ant-hill with a magnifying glass – and I'm the ant.' Yet grace comes through the film, as Bruce is granted 'divine powers' – and when he asks why such a gift is given to him, God responds, 'That's the beauty of it – you can ask why.' The ability to question is seen as a grace gift.

And the agony of grace ignored is explored, as Bruce/God laments, 'How do you make someone love you?' Grace, as Yancey astutely comments, is 'what the world thirsts for.' Can the Christian church bring cool water to such parched lips? Those who live in a grace-less desert are waiting:

> In our day heaven and earth are on tiptoe waiting for the emergence of a Spirit-led, Spirit intoxicated, Spirit empowered people. All of creation watches expectantly for the springing up of a disciplined, freely gathered, martyr people who know in this life the life and power of the kingdom of God. It has happened before. It can happen again … Such a people will not emerge until there is among us a deeper, more profound experience of an Emmanuel of the Spirit – God with us, a knowledge that in the power of the Spirit Jesus has come to guide his people himself, an experience of His leading that is as definite and as immediate as the cloud by day and the fire by night.[4]

Grace must thus be let out of the church ghetto: it will affect our stance in so many current, difficult issues. Grace will shape our attitude to asylum seekers, who have become an easy target for media driven rage in the call for the preservation of 'our' resources. When grace is around, our eyes will see people with disabilities in an altogether different light, as grace shatters the myth of 'normality' and 'basic wholeness'. All of us, able bodied or otherwise, stand in need before God, and all of us carry equal value. We deserve to be seen as individuals, not characterised by our primary, obvious challenges, as designations

---

[4] John Ortberg, *The Life you've always wanted*, (Zondervan, 2003)

like 'the disabled' do. Instead, grace teaches us to look for the image of God that is to be found in all. The way that we treat people with disabilities in our listening, in our language, and in responding to the need for access becomes a grace issue, and not just one of political correctness. And grace will cause us to redefine what success really is: the publishing of tables that score and rate our schools has perhaps contributed to an examination pressure that is premature (young children 'graduating' from play into study too early) and an oppressive 'achiever' culture that measures worth only in terms of academic prowess. The truth about grace is pertinent to so many issues of life.

> GRACE MUST BE
> LET OUT OF THE
> CHURCH GHETTO

Grace for choices

The suggestion that we need to make choices about grace could be misleading. In this world of self-help books, one might get the impression that it all hinges with us, with our abilities to select the right paths and follow through on our decisions. So we must know that it takes grace even to be able to make a good choice in the first place. The grace of God is the source of the revelations, insights and moments of inspiration that prompt us to choose rightly in the first place. And of course, we will need grace if our choices are to be followed through with any kind of consistency and be anything more than spiritual wishful thinking.

None the less, Scripture is loaded with moments when God invited people – and nations – to make choices. His help was at hand when they did, but he refused to override what is one of the basic privileges of being human; the ability to decide. Those days of decision were usually rudder-like moments that shaped their future destiny. Much hinged on the moment of choice.

My experience as a Christian, these last thirty years, is that the ability to choose is what makes the difference between a disciple who moves forward in steady growth and faithfulness and the one who 'makes shipwreck' of their faith.

Kay and I have recently become friends with Debra Veal, who hit the headlines when she rowed the Atlantic Ocean alone not long ago. That feat (described in the excellent book *Rowing it alone*[5]) had been done before, but what made the story remarkable was the fact that Debra kept going even though the crossing had never been intended as a solo endeavour. She had planned to participate in the race with her husband Andrew, but it became apparent after just a few days that he would not be able to complete the journey. He made the brave decision to concede this: and she made the courageous choice to carry on alone. Over one hundred days later, her skin bronzed from the sun, her calf muscles so wasted that she had to learn how to balance and walk again, she arrived triumphantly, to the delight of her family and a watching world. She had braved close encounters with sharks, smaller discomforts like running out of toilet paper half way across

[5] Debra Veal, *Rowing it alone – One woman's extraordinary transatlantic adventure* (Robson Books, 2002)

the pond, and the unexpected bruising of flying fish smashing into her as she rowed on alone: but she did it. An overnight guest in our home recently, Debra told us that choice was a big key. She had a little card with the words *Choose your attitude* written on it, and the card was displayed in a prominent place in that tiny boat. I wonder how many hundreds of times she glanced at that simple, profound saying – and decided that bad attitudes were not allowed onboard. Debra would be the first to say that grace played a huge part in getting her through what might have been an ordeal, but was an adventure for her – but that grace came as she decided, as she chose her emotional posture each day. Something similar can happen to us in our journeying: as grace prompts us, we decide, and as we decide, grace helps us forward.

> CHOOSE YOUR
> ATTITUDE

What choices are being be prompted in you?

And if, even through the pages of this book, God nudges us, when will you and I begin to take action? Procrastination is a subtle temptation to the Christian, particularly as we are prone to believe that God speaking to us and challenging us is of merit in itself, whether or not we actually take any notice of what he has said. We can live our whole lives in the future, a kind of postponed existence, indefinitely preparing to live, and promising ourselves that joy is just a little way ahead of us. But tomorrow never comes. Or we can spend our days looking back over our shoulders, living in regret, in rose tinted reminiscences, fooling ourselves that the days gone by were surely better than what is or what is to come. But God wants us to be people of today, of this moment: planning for the future, grateful for what was good yesterday, but determined to know him, hear him and make grace choices – today.

Find the wonder again

It is also my prayer that the words that follow will perhaps stir us to a reawakened sense of wonder about grace: that those of us who have been around Christianity for more than a few years, and for whom faith is something of an old habit, will find ourselves once again open-mouthed at the sheer splendour of it all. May we move away from a Christian life that is merely habitual and unexciting, and be surprised at the very core of ourselves once more.

If grace is the music that the world needs to hear, then we need to unstop our ears to listen once again to its lilting melody, and dance to its delightful rhythm. Robert Farrar Capon provides a loving challenge:

> Grace is the celebration of life, relentlessly hounding all the non-celebrants in the world. It is a floating, cosmic bash shouting its way through the streets of the universe, flinging the sweetness of its cessations to every window, pounding at every door in a hilarity beyond all liking and happening, until the prodigals come out at last and dance, and the elder brothers finally take their fingers out of their ears.[6]

---

[6] Robert Farrar Capon, *Parables of Grace*, (Wm B Eerdmans, 1990)

Let's take our fingers out of *our* ears, and ask the Holy Spirit to teach us once more how to dance along to his song.

Jeff Lucas
Colorado 2004

1

I WILL ALLOW MY VISION OF GOD TO BE SHAPED BY GRACE

Grace, indeed, is beauty in action
Disraeli

He stared down at me, his eyes wide and fixed. His thin lips were pressed tightly together, no hint of a smile. The face was white, with not a blush of colour anywhere – was this the white of purity, or the chalky mask of death? I peered through the flickering candle-light and tried to look deeper into those eyes. Was it my imagination, or did I just glimpse a softening, the slightest narrowing of those fixed eyelids, into something other than a glare? Did those pursed lips curl ever so slightly upwards? Perhaps not. His eyes were hollow, and his nose was long, and he stared down it like a judge about to pass sentence. Yet those eyes bored through me: he surely knew the worst; all my secrets. The blood on his brow was congealed, muddy brown rather than bright crimson: old blood, a dribble from a wound inflicted long ago, in another world, by other people.

He held his arms out to me: and for a moment, I felt a glimmer of hope. Was he beckoning me, inviting me to come closer into the warmth of an embrace? Or was he like a policeman signalling traffic to halt – holding his hands out to warn me to keep my distance? Back off, sinner boy, don't cross the threshold. I watched him, conscious that others had sat right where I sat now for over a thousand years, and they had watched him too.

Had they, like me, dared him to move? Had he ever smiled at *them*? What could stir him?

BACK OFF, SINNER BOY

I decided to try a little provocation, bringing to my mind a swear word, and repeating it in my head, challenging him to react, as surely he would be able to read my profane thoughts. Still, like a big bland holy puppet, he stared down at me. Nothing.

I shivered but not from the cold; stood and grabbed my coat. Then I paused to cross myself quickly – more superstition than devotion. Eager to get out of there now, my hurried steps echoed down the nave. I fumbled for the big, iron door handle, and walked out into the welcome afternoon sun, leaving Jesus behind – or rather, the stained glass image of him that dominated the altar area. I left him marooned in the twilight that ruled in that musty old place. I didn't want anything to do with *him*. He looked too much like a glowing prefect, a pompous moralist who could never be satisfied, no matter how good I might become. I ran more than walked to the gate, bolting it firmly behind me. I was glad to leave him back there in that half light, alone, and still staring.

It would be another five years before I bumped into him again, and this time, it was quite an unexpected meeting. It wasn't even a church building where I found him – but in a classroom of a newly built comprehensive school. The smell of fresh paint lingered in the air, a constant reminder that we were the privileged pupils who got to be the first to use this beautiful, untried building.

The class was about religion – GCE Religious Education in fact: but it was not in the curriculum that I noticed him, but in the eyes – and the life – of the teacher. Mrs Richardson was a rushing, mildly panicked woman. A committed Christian, and a minister's wife, it seemed that she was always being put upon by other staff members because she seemed so very willing to serve. She dashed from classroom to classroom, delivering lessons, solving head-of-year hassles, and then finding time to lead the weekly Christian Union meeting before rushing home to become a pastor's wife once again. And when she talked about Jesus, it was captivating: for her, the blood on his forehead was still bright crimson, his sufferings still mattered, his resurrection real. He was her friend. I wanted to meet him, and so wandered along to the Christian Union, under the pretence that I had come to disrupt it and steal the biscuits. Within weeks, I became a follower of Christ.

I did so, because I had been treated to a glimpse of the real God – and his kindness and grace – through the working model that was the life of that woman. Her life, though surely imperfect, had been changed by his grace rhythm; I wanted to get in step too. Sadly, too many people have never had such a privileged opportunity as I. They have decided to reject what they see as a very odd and irrelevant person called God: but really they have rejected a hideous facsimile of him. That's not to say that the *real* Jesus has not been rejected many times: it's

impossible really to live *without* him, and sometimes it's terribly difficult to live *with* him. But the godlet that I had ?
turned my back on was not whom I later found: I reject-
ed an imitation; a mutation; a freak.

Many others have done the same: they have turned their back, not on the real God, but on the God they perceive him to be. God has been ruthlessly caricatured, his appear-ance twisted by humanity into a million grotesque pictures; false images created, for example, by the chequered history of the church. When the church fails, God is found guilty by association.

SOMETIMES IT
IS TERRIBLY
DIFFICULT TO LIVE
WITH HIM

It may be difficult for us to connect with the atrocities of history, but we must try, lest we repeat yesterday's mistakes. Look at the blood-letting of the Crusades and then try to think of God, and he appears to be the author of limitless ethnic cleansing, deaf to the cries of thousands for mercy. Imagine the screams of those tormented by thumbscrew and rack during the stain on church history that was the Inquisition, and God looks like a grinning sadist. God's reputation has suffered at the hands of those who have thought that they 'owned' him – and in justify-ing their cruelty by using his Name as a licence, they acted as if they did think that. The church always becomes an evil force when it begins to think that it has the franchise for the divine. And the scandals of history are repeated daily in many more subtle ways. Untold damage is done as some Christian leaders, with measured tones and convincing proof texts, paint a credible but false portrait of God. However winsome the preaching, the fact is that it may well create yet another picture that bears little or no resemblance to the truth. Such is the potential that we all have to make the Bible say whatever we want it to say.

After a while, exhausted and disappointed by the weekly freak show, Christians leave the church. And no wonder. The unthinking, legalistic parent who condemns their child's fashion and music choices, bundling them all into a refuse skip called 'worldliness' without thinking through the issues – or explaining them to the child – creates

HOW EASILY WE MAKE GOD INTO A MONSTER

another ugly lesion in the face of God, a warped vision that may well drive them away both from God and church.

How easily we make God into a monster or a bore in turn. How many have rejected a dull God, fearing that he might just be the spitting image of the frigid congregation that claims to know him. In a rigid understanding of holiness and transcendence, we have lost sight of the wonderful news that there is a Person at the heart of all things who is the very best, the highest example of nobility and self sacrifice, the epitome of patience, love and kindness – and the most saintly human is but a pale reflection of him.

Sometimes casual words deface him. While I remain convinced that the Bible teaches heaven and hell as realities, we would do well to think through carefully what those words really mean, lest we misuse them and do great damage. The Dante-inspired medieval vision of Hades, resplendent with fork-toting demons and unquenchable fires may well have caused many to reject God out of hand as a divine commandant of the worst concentration camp that has ever been: and in this vista of a post-life Auschwitz, the crematorium chimneys belch smoke forever.

It is obvious that these caricatures systematically build great obstacles to mission: why would people want to respond to the invitation to turn to the One they view as a vicious, heartless despot? Pete Gilbert, a good friend and a gifted evangelist, has recently written a book called *Kiss and Tell*.[1] Pete sees evangelism as the art of learning to 'kiss' God in worship and friendship, and then pass the wonderful news about that encounter on: surely a lovely analogy. But who would want to kiss a monster?

God has been disguised, his beauty masked. Perhaps that is why Dietrich Bonhoeffer said that the church's main task is to 'wash the face of Jesus', to remove the religious grime with which he has been smeared – most often by the church – over the years. The real shining face of Jesus will be, to many, irresistible – if they could only get a glimpse of it.

What has all of this to do with our ability to know and experience grace? I will repeat what I said earlier: grace will not be renewed in us simply as we learn cold information about God, but rather as we allow him to renew our experience of him, and alter our vision of him – the beautiful One. Grace is far more than an abstract (or impersonal) theological idea; it flows from the wonderful reality that God is truly the essence of authentic

---

[1] Pete Gilbert, *Kiss and Tell*, (CWR, 2003)

beauty. Grace is not discovered by merely considering what God *does*, but rather as we encounter *who he is*: it is rooted in his character, and not just his activities. So, when the Scripture seeks to communicate that God epitomizes love, it takes a step forward from simply announcing that he does loving things or acts with love: rather, we are told, 'God *is* love'.[2]

Everything that he does – and all that he is – is entwined with loving kindness and grace. Grace is no mere force or special commodity; it is not impersonal magic, a sparkly spell or transforming moon dust.

GRACE IS FOUND IN THE ONE WHO IS GRACIOUS

Grace is more than a kiss from Prince Charming or the waving of a wand – rather, grace is found in the One who is gracious. All of which makes the outrages of yesteryear, perpetuated in his Name, the more scandalous.

But in 'washing the face of Jesus', we must be wary of a more subtle, fashionable masking of the true God – as we apply humanistic make-up, and produce an air-brushed, new-improved God for the delight of the grinning throng. We must not try to revise him because we do not understand him, or worse because we do comprehend but don't like what he does. To look at him will always require the trust that alone will lead us through the fogbanks of mystery that inevitably surround him as we peer at him from this side of heaven.

We can be guilty of smearing his face with the rouge of sentimentality, applying a softer, more acceptable hue to him. Or we cake the make-up on when we attempt to

---

[2] 1 John 4:8, 16

understand him only in human terms – reducing him to someone that we can fully comprehend or control. As the book title reminds us, the illusion of a manageable deity is dangerous.[3]

Ironically, some have even diminished the truth of grace in their quest to make God more palatable. There are those who insist that all of humanity will ultimately be saved, regardless of their response to the gospel: universalism. They actually turn God into one who will force himself upon as all at the end of things, tossing away our ability to choose and hauling us all into the captivity of heaven. Such 'love' is no love at all, as it strips us of our freedom of choice and turns heaven into something forced upon us, an eternal violation. And not only that: the idea is an unbiblical one! The fact remains that there will be many things about God that will continue to make us uncomfortable: nonetheless we must allow God to be who he is; God.

> GOD IS
> BEAUTIFUL

All that qualified and said, the fact remains that God is beautiful – and not many people know that. Grace is only really experienced as we turn to see that the author of it is indeed 'the fairest of ten thousand'. Our perception of who God is governs the way that we live, and certainly the way that we live with him: it shapes everything about the way we 'do' Christianity. Surely all of us need to pray constantly that we will know God in truth, as he is, rather than unwittingly worshipping an object partly made of our own creation, a tapestry woven from

[3] D W McCullough, *The Trivialization of God: the dangerous illusion of a manageable deity* (Navpress, 1995)

the myriad strands of our own upbringing, a few hundred sermons and our hopes and fears – perhaps the sum total of all of our experience to date. We will never have a pure, utterly biblical view of God this side of eternity – our humanity will ensure that – but we can pray that God will purify and change that vision, as we address our prayers not to who we think God is but to whom God knows himself to be. Grace is rooted in us knowing the True, Beautiful One – which is one reason in many why it is vital that we know Scripture. When his character is assaulted, we will have no defence to hand if we are not armed with a solid understanding of the Bible.

Journeying into beauty

Sharing a little about my own conversion could give the impression that I suddenly saw the light about the true nature of God and that I was instantly struck by his beauty: all negative images were swept away in a moment. And that would have been very nice – but it certainly didn't happen that way. Perhaps that's why I continue to be a little nervous of that phrase that Christians occasionally use in sharing their own stories: 'I came to know the Lord.' It's as if there was some instant encounter with the divine that was so epic that it deleted all of the negative perceptions they had accumulated about him through years of misunderstanding; so that, in a moment, they had a revelation of a far greater and more gracious version of God. It certainly wasn't that way for me.

The early years of my Christian life were exciting, but nerve-racking, as I felt like a whipped puppy, frequently flinching and living in daily expectation that I would be judged. That wide eyed, staring chap on the cross still haunted me, especially in meetings where there was a wide eyed, staring chap in the pulpit. Providentially, the minister of the church that I attended was a warm, laugh-out-loud type; his eyes sparkled with an infectious love for God. Nevertheless, I became totally paranoid about repentance, and would occasionally go forward seeking forgiveness for things that weren't sin. Films and books about the second coming were the rage back then, and so most shopping trips would include an episode of me being parted from Kay in a shop. I would then dash around the place frantically searching for her, convinced that she had been taken up into the clouds to meet with Jesus, and I, of course, the rampant sinner, had been left behind. I really thought that she had been transported in vertical take off to heaven, but usually she was found in the more ordinary environment of the ladies' underwear section. But the point was this: I always expected to be the one discarded from the second coming: that old vision of God, just brimming with anticipation at the thought of judging me, lingered on.

And that somewhat ugly vision affected so much of my decision making. Learning that there was something called 'the will of God for my life', I decided to try to find it. Much agonising and heart searching followed: but the old vision of God seemed clearly to infer that God's perfect will for me was probably going to be rather painful. I saw God as a distant dentist, leaning over my mouth with a huge set of pliers, muttering, 'This is going to hurt you a lot more than it hurts me, my child.' I thus concluded that, since I had no desire whatsoever to become a missionary, stamping around steaming jungles sharing tracts with head hunters, that this was most likely what the Lord would have me do. And the decision to marry Kay was difficult, because she was – and is – a very attractive lady. Surely the dentist above would have me marry someone whom I found utterly unattractive, or so I mused. Readers familiar with my looks may conclude that Kay also believed that perverse doctrine. The idea that the will of God would be good – and by that I mean,

❧ ☙

I SAW GOD
AS A DISTANT
DENTIST

❧ ☙

enjoyable rather than just good for me, like a foul tasting cough medicine – just didn't occur to me. My approach to the every day was shaped by my stunted vision of God, and that didn't change overnight. Indeed, the journey into a renewed vision of him continues to this day.

God, truly the beautiful One

> 'One thing I ask of the LORD, this is what I seek: that I may dwell in the house of the LORD all the days of my life, to *gaze upon the beauty of the* LORD and to seek him in his temple.'[4]

God has always been beautiful and full of grace – which comes as a surprise to some who seem to think that the rather difficult God of the Old Testament attended an Alpha course, straightened up and became a nice

---

[4] Psalm 27:4

Christian God in the New! But the Old Testament provides us with a rich and multi-layered portrait of the beautiful God: he is the genius Creator, the maker of the intricate, varied and imaginative triumph that is creation itself. He is the source of life to all, in his lavish offering of common grace, as all of creation has always been sustained daily and enriched by his tending and empowering. Rainfall and sunshine flow from his hand; he is good both to the atheist and the believer.

RAINFALL AND SUNSHINE FLOW FROM HIS HAND

Even in judgement, his kindness is evident, as in his 'making garments of skin' for the ashamed first couple. His generosity is demonstrated in his willingness to give away authority, calling Adam and Eve to participate in the naming of creation, and the patriarchs to participate in his adventure. He gives the law, which was an act of grace – a surprise to some who see law and grace as antithetical. His tender heart is melted for the poor and the oppressed, and demonstrates consistent love for 'little' Israel. Bountiful forgiveness is offered through tearful prophets, and he shows compassion even for 'heathen' Nineveh. The Psalmist searches for language sufficiently rich to celebrate his steadfast love.

The subject of grace is so vast, so comprehensive, that even to consider any kind of exploration of 'the incomparable riches of God's grace'[5] is like opening the door of a bank vault, only to discover that it is miles wide. Grace has touched every second of pre-history, human history, and will pervade eternity.

---

[5] Ephesians 2:7

And the melody of grace is even louder and clearer in the New Testament, where grace is now seen in the foreground, and is offered to the wider world beyond Israel. The grace hope of the Old Testament is now fulfilled in the coming of Christ.

Jesus exuded grace. In Luke's record, grace rested upon him from infancy and subsequently he grew in grace, spoke gracious words, and passed unharmed through a hostile mob. Now in him, grace *is* outrageous, because it is given at the prerogative of God to the undeserving through the scandal of the cross.

JESUS EXUDED GRACE

His forgiveness is beautiful, in that it leads us way beyond legal pardon, into friendship with himself. He is the transforming sculptor who can take the marred mess of us and make us into something like himself. His tenderness is ours, offering sustenance during trial, wisdom to the confounded and confused, signs to the lost, boldness to the fearful, and strength to the tempted. Indeed, every step in the process of the Christian life is due to grace – our own talents and abilities are but fruits of grace at work in us. And, ultimately, grace 'will lead us home': in John's Gospel, the idea of grace is related to eternal life. Eternity for the Christian is not just endless existence, but it is being with Jesus, as part of the redeemed community, and experiencing his eternal kindness. When we consider God's beauty, we consider the consistent song of Scripture.

But the word 'beauty' is itself in need of some redemption: it is a rich word that has been hijacked and glossed in recent years. Beauty has become synonymous with glamour, which it is not. Quite obviously a person may be attractive in appearance, and yet be truly deformed because of their selfish behaviour or bitter obsessions. When it comes to beauty, God is Spirit, and therefore physical comeliness is an irrelevance, but his matchless beauty is none the less discovered in the exquisite nature of his personhood. And his beauty is not associated with the traditional male forms of strength: on the contrary, his beauty is mingled with and indeed rooted in vulnerability – as a choice that he has willingly made, and continues to make.

> ≈ ≈
>
> HE IS STUNNING IN HIS SERVANT-WEAKNESS
>
> ≈ ≈

Beauty and weakness

'He had no beauty or majesty to attract us to him....'[6]

The beauty of God is most profoundly seen in that he is the bloodied, yet victorious rescuer. On the Cross, Jesus became a truly ugly and gory object of scorn: and yet the strange sight of him at Calvary is the most awesome sight that there has ever been. He is stunning in his servant-weakness.

This issue is far more than an item of theological nicety; the portrait of beautiful weakness is a vision that empowers marginalised people. Those who would be tagged as ugly, as nerds and losers, by a culture that worships superficial beauty, can now find the best seats at the banquet. People with

---

[6] Isaiah 53:2

disabilities have often found themselves disenfranchised and rejected by the 'able' crowd. But the revelation of God made beautiful in the chosen weakness
of incarnation and crucifixion has been a eye-opener
to many.

Nancy Eisland, the American writer on disability and
religion, records a moment of personal revelation about
God:

> I saw God in a sip-puff wheelchair, that is, the chair
> used mostly by quadriplegics, enabling them to
> manoeuvre by blowing and sucking on a straw-like
> device. Not an omnipotent self-sufficient God, but
> neither a pitiable suffering servant. In this moment,
> I beheld God as a survivor, unpitying and forthright. I
> recognised the incarnate Christ in the image of those
> judged 'not feasible', 'unemployable', with 'question-
> able quality of life.' Here was God for me.[7]

Grace comes as we see afresh that God is 'for me' – 'for
us' – that he has travelled such a distance, has gone
through such unspeakable pain, and has become so vul-
nerable in order to call us to himself. This is a true,
bloody beauty, even if a vision of God in a wheelchair is
strong stuff for us to consider.

He is beautiful, not because he became weak as an
unwitting victim, but because he *chose* to embrace 'disability' in his endless pursuit of us. And paradoxically,
in that place of weakness we see his great strength – but
then isn't it true that the 'weakest' people are often those
who are truly the strongest, because their harrowing

---

[7] Nancy L Eisland, *The Disabled God: towards a Liberatory
Theology of Disability* (Nashville: Abingdon press, 1994), p89

experiences have given them moral muscle that most of us can only dream about?

True beauty: welcoming the 'losers'

I am totally biased, I know, but I think that Kelly, our daughter, is very beautiful. The sound of her laughter or the hint of her smile never fails to send the clouds away from me. But what makes her especially dazzling in my fatherly eyes is her heart for the bruised and broken, her dedication to speaking up for those who cannot defend themselves. It's a passion that's been with her from her earliest years, has taken her to some very deprived and dark areas of the globe, and has fuelled her university studies in development. Her husband, Ben, is made of the same stuff, running play schemes for children in Kosovo, in the stifling heat of East Timor, and in the orphanages of Romania, where he has had a part in teaching little ones who grew up too soon to giggle again.

My favourite photograph of Kelly is of her hugging a little Romanian girl, Ana-Maria – a member of a family that has suffered horrendous abuse. Her brother had lines slashed across his face, the handiwork of a drunken mother who decided to play with a razor blade and her son's soft skin. She is serving a prison sentence for her outrageous evil, which included amputating some of his fingers. Knowing the background of horror that these children suffered, the photograph is harrowing, yet quite lovely – what courage and true joy beams from the little girl's eyes – and Kelly never looked so beautiful as when she is captured reaching out to those who have been so cruelly marginalised.

A portrait of One who is whole reaching out to the broken is found in the biblical photograph of our God, as we see his insistence on touching the last, the least and the lost. In human relationships, like often attracts like. The handsome and the gorgeous herd together in school, leaving the less attractive and unathletic out in the cold, branded always as the uncool. Not so with God: his true beauty shines in his heart for the people on the edges, as he comes as a physician to tend to the sick – which, in truth, means all of us.

GOD GIVES WHERE HE FINDS EMPTY HANDS

We can only enter the kingdom on the basis of acknowledging that we are all, in a sense, 'losers' – whatever our natural abilities or accomplishments, we just don't 'have the goods' to make the grade with God. On the contrary, God's people are those who know that they will only gain a pass through the One who has passed the test for us all. Those who see themselves as self-sufficient 'winners' are unable even to enter God's grace school. As Augustine said so memorably, 'God gives where He finds empty hands.' So, count yourself in. Grace is a call to every one of us: none are excluded.

And why not pray often that God might take you on a renewed journey of discovery, one that will renew your vision and perception of who he is? Ask the Holy Spirit to strip away masks that have been placed quietly over the Father's face over the years, disfiguring him, and making it difficult for you to draw near to him with peace. That vision will be sharpened as we choose to soak our hearts and minds in Scripture. It will be renewed by our deciding to live thankful lives: his beauty shines as it is celebrated. And perhaps we need to rediscover the power of testimony in our churches, as we proclaim to one another the story of God and his part in our stories.

Find gracious people, and hang out with them. Their loveliness will inspire and shape your own vision of God. Be bold enough to see that not every portrait that we have seen of him is true – and some of us have been drip fed a diet of lies. Be courageous enough to question. A vision shaped by grace will demand that there are some false portraits that need to be systematically deleted from our hearts and minds.

Walking in a greater sense of grace begins with us seeing afresh a biblical vision of the God who truly is beautiful, the One so stunning that he is, 'the glorious One – who lifts up my head.'[8]

---

[8] Psalm 3:3

2

I WILL CHOOSE TO BELIEVE THAT GOD IS PASSIONATE ABOUT ME

God is not cool and collected but is deeply
involved and can be wounded.
Clark Pinnock

God, who is the origin of our emotions and who
created our emotions, certainly does feel emotions.
Wayne Grudem

Abandoned and bowed down

Some years ago, I went to see my doctor for my annual physical check-up. I've told the story of that most embarrassing event elsewhere, but permit me to repeat it here, because it paints a word picture that I feel could help us as we consider the issue of grace choices further.

Dr. Chris is also my best friend, and so the examination had been littered with ribald comments and much mocking of what I think is my finely honed physique. No one likes to be prodded and poked around, and suffer the indignity of nakedness before close friends, so I was eager, desperate even, to get out of that clinic. One little treat remained: I had to have a chest x-ray. I wandered, semi-clad, down the hallway, found a room that had a welcoming 'radiation – danger' sign on the door, and stepped into one of the most excruciating episodes of my life. A strong statement, I know, seeing that I sometimes feel like a Bible-clutching Mr. Bean, staggering as I do from one gaffe to another for the apparent entertainment of the Christian public – but this was truly one of the most embarrassing of those episodes.

Inside the room stood a smiling radiologist, waiting in readiness beside the expected x-ray machine. There was a couch, and spread on the couch was a lead apron that weighed around thirty pounds. I was nervous, agitated, and not really listening, so I muttered, 'What's the apron for?'

'It is for the protection of the gonads,' she replied with another smile. I nodded my understanding, which was a lie. Gonads? What were they? An obscure North American Indian tribe? The people who lived next door to the doctor's clinic, Mr and Mrs Gonad, who surely needed shielding from errant radioactive waves?

She was obviously unaware of my anatomical ignorance, and was also in need of a cup of coffee, so I *thought* she said, as she left the room in search of caffeine, 'Put that around your neck.' Of course, I now know too well that she actually said *waist*. In my flustered state, I wasn't focused, so I heard *neck*.

I try to do what I am told. I picked up the rather heavy apron, hauled it up onto my chest, and tied the tapes together around my neck in one large, attractive bow. The solid weight hung down, seeming heavier by the second as I hunched over. I was unable to move, unable to look up, unable to do anything other than sweat. Profusely. And pray. And the irony was, I had found myself in this state because *I thought that I was following the right instructions*, surely a parable in itself for those who have been raised on a rigid diet of ungrace.

I prayed that the radiologist would come back. I prayed that the Lord Jesus would come back, but neither responded. She was busy making coffee, and he was busy running the universe, so I stood there, in pain, alone. No criticism is implied for the kindly radiologist at all – she was only gone for a couple of minutes, and if I had listened to her carefully, then I wouldn't have been in the position in the first place. But for what seemed a long while, I felt like no one was interested in my predicament. She finally walked back into the room, clutching a steaming cup of coffee. She took one look at me, resisted the temptation to laugh out loud, and simply said, 'No...' Within seconds I was relieved of my self-imposed burden; the sun came out, life was good again. Someone cared, and I was able to stand upright once more.

A RIGID DIET OF UNGRACE

But there have been a few times when I have found myself in a place where it seemed that God wasn't on hand to help me – and didn't really care too much about me anyway. Ironically, some of these sticky moments of despair came when I actually thought I was being obedient and following the Maker's instructions. But it seemed that he was absent, aloof, indifferent to my plight. Even if he saw the jam I was in, he wasn't overly concerned. I was very wrong: but the notion of a dispassionate, emotionally detached God can linger, with serious consequences.

Nothing's changed in heaven?

The time of worship had been an enjoyable experience: I took a peek over my shoulder and surveyed the people behind me. It seemed that the gathering of ministers for their annual retreat had brought together a group eager to worship. This was encouraging, as sometimes those who are responsible for the weekly overseeing of worship services unwittingly start to view praising God as 'work': not something to be too keen on when you're having a few days off. But this group seemed more than willing to participate with energy: some knelt; others lifted hands aloft, while still others sat quietly and enjoyed the atmosphere.

Suddenly, the worship leader came to the end of a song, and decided to share a few thoughts. We listened, and he began to talk about the tragedy that was the Columbine School shootings. I live just a few miles away from Columbine High School in Littleton, just outside Denver, Colorado. It was there on April 20, 1999, that Eric Harris and Dylan Klebold murdered twelve students and a teacher during a killing spree that lasted but a few minutes. Shock waves reverberated around Colorado and, indeed, the world when those young lives were so mercilessly snuffed out.

The worship leader told us how stunned he had been at this tragedy, and how, devastated, he had gone to the Lord in prayer about the situation. But then he shared what he perceived God said in response to his prayers. 'Nothing has changed in heaven', was the one sentence that was apparently God's helpful quip about the slaughter of those innocents. My mouth fell open. Perhaps this

comment was intended to reassure us that God is beyond
the reach of a crazed gunman's bullets, (as indeed he is),
or that, ultimately, God's plan for planet earth rolls forward uninterrupted by such tragedies, in the mystery of
his sovereignty. But I confess that what the now smiling
worship leader shared as a word of encouragement left
me quite numbed, giving as it did
the impression of a God aloof,
unable to enter into the suffering   HE SURELY IS THE
that that day had created.   PASSIONATE ONE

I took my seat, placed my heads
in my hands, and struggled to make
sense of what I had just heard. Worship suddenly
became extremely difficult; adoration of such an uncar-
ing, passionless God almost impossible. Once again, let
me affirm that we must never succumb to the temptation to anthropomorphise God and make him after the
image of our choosing – and that's certainly not what I
am advocating here – but this portrait of such an unfeel-
ing deity seemed – and seems – so out of kilter with the
biblical revelation of the God who is revealed to us in
Christ Jesus. He surely is the passionate One: (a statement that needs qualification, but is none the less true);
such passion is the fuel of grace. Grace is a quickened,
urgent heartbeat rather than a measured, cool stare: the
grace of God causes him to throw open his heart to all of
our ugliness and loveliness. Surely a cocooned God,
distant from us and our little pains, is not One who is so
very gracious? Perhaps we can be guilty of a pharisaic
view of God: the three 'lost' parables (the stories about
the coin, the sheep and the prodigal) each end with a
celebratory party. Jesus told these stories with an eye on

the ever-murmuring Pharisees in the crowd, who were unhappy about his mixing with sinners. They seemed to worship a God who was more a judge than a father: one ever 'keeping the score', ready to pass sentence, rather than the father who throws extravagant parties and says 'we had to celebrate'. Our ability to experience God's grace is surely dependant on our capacity to expect that he would – and will – throw similar parties for us, such is his passion for us. Of course, all of this can sound a little too good to be true – like a Christian fairy tale...

The Knight's Tale

The classic 'damson in distress' story is familiar enough: a gorgeous but sadly helpless blonde is held captive in the summit of a turreted tower. She is the prisoner of an evil, leering despot who plans to have his wicked way with her and then kill her. She screams and wails into the night, hoping against hope that some passing gallant chap will help her out. Enter, cavalry-like, our hero knight in appropriately buffed and therefore shining armour. He has travelled thousands of miles on his sweating but trusty steed: together they have crossed rivers infested with razor-toothed piranhas, they have scaled Everest-like slopes, have fought off entire armies single-handed, and all because of one thing that burns in the heart of Sir Knight; passion.

So utterly, desperately, and urgently does he love the fair maiden, that nothing can stand in the way of his rescue mission. At last our hero climbs the sheer face of the tower, kills the evil oppressor with one hand and pulls the tearful beauty to his warm embrace with the other. As the orchestra builds to a romantic crescendo, we are left in no doubt: it was no calm, calculating man who conquered the hills and the waves and even the passing piranhas: rather it was a man of passion who endured it all in order to be the deliverer. Passion has triumphed.

Beautiful; but it's a fictional tale. Or is it? The Bible teaches that the love and grace of God caused him to launch the greatest rescue mission that there has ever been, and one certainly involving the longest journey in the history of journeys; mind-boggling descriptions of trillions of light years between stars fade into nothingness when compared with the distance navigated in the incarnation. The gap between the throne of God and the stable of Bethlehem is surely the widest chasm, certainly in terms of contrast, that there has ever been. But what motivated such a journey, if it was not passion? Mark Stibbe comments on the passion and pain of that mission: 'The Father loves us with a selfless passion. The word passion comes from a Latin word that means suffering. The Father's love for us is a love that costs, that hurts, that suffers.'[1]

THE GREATEST RESCUE MISSION THAT THERE HAS EVER BEEN

Thus many Christians speak of the cross and the Easter event as *The Passion* – of a bloodied grace that has sweated and groaned to win us. Mel Gibson's *The Passion of The Christ*, a film that depicts the harrowing violence that Jesus suffered during his last few hours,

---

[1] Mark Stibbe, *From Orphans to Heirs: celebrating our spiritual adoption*, (BRF, 1999)

has created considerable controversy. I have yet to see the film, but plan to do so, as it seems that Gibson has created a cinematic portrayal of the sufferings of Christ that is loaded with the blood, sweat and tears of true passion. When we think of the cross, have we developed a vision of a sanitised, inoffensive, passionless Passion? The cross is surely the great sob of God. 'The crucified Jesus is the only accurate picture of God the world has ever seen.'[2] At the cross, we see God as he chooses to have us see him – not the all powerful, impervious Creator, but the bloodied, beaten Saviour, gulping for air, stretching himself up on a tiny wooden shelf to try to prevent his lungs from filling with blood, and thus from drowning. There we see the agony of the Father, turning away from his Son at his most desperate moment of need, shunning him, that he might be able to welcome us. Where but at the cross do we see more graphically what Kazoh Kitamori has aptly described as the 'pain of God'? In the cross of Christ, a rupture tears, as it were, through God himself.

THE CROSS IS SURELY THE GREAT SOB STORY OF GOD

Yet some seem uncomfortable with the thought that there is real passion in the person of God: they are nervous about the idea that God can be truly moved, grieved, excited or ecstatic. There are some – very few – would want us to see God as the One who cannot be moved at all, which turns him into a metaphysical block

---

[2] John Austin Baker

of ice. They paint a portrait of a God who is apathetic, an unmoved and stern papa. One ultra-high Calvinist wrote these astonishing words: 'God has no desires and no affections, no true delight or grief, and certainly no sorrow over anything that comes to pass – because his mind is pure, sovereign, irresistible will.'[3]

While most refuse such a truncated view of God, still some struggle with the idea that passion really pulses in the divine heart. The fruit of this is that, when I searched on the internet using the words 'passion of God', I discovered hundreds (if not thousands) of articles about how we should have passion in our pursuit of God, but very little about *him* having passion for *us*!

Sadly, theological debates about this issue have produced a lot more heat than light: 'classical theists' and 'open theists' have caricatured each others' positions in discussions, and sometimes diatribes, that have raged on through years of church history. I will not trouble you with the details here: suffice it to say that the discussion centres around the doctrine of impassibility: which, pushed to an extreme, is the idea that God is untouched by pain – or indeed anything at all. He is securely and consistently 'blessed' (most happy) because nothing can affect his condition or bring a shadow to his day. If he is the ultimate constant, then nothing can change him – and therefore he must be impervious to being affected by any external influence or emotion. In reality, that is not what the doctrine is

---

[3] Noted in the internet article based on 'God without mood swings – recovering the doctrine of divine impassibility' – Philip R Johnson, excerpted from Douglas Wilson (Ed.), *Bound only once*, (Canon Press, 2001)

really trying to say, but sadly, some have interpreted it to mean that God is without passion. This God is disinterested; wounded once by my sin, but untouched by it now. God lives in happy resignation.[4] Such a vision of God seems icy cold at best – and mildly psychopathic at worst: a portrait of ugliness surely.

What kind of lover is God if he loves without passion and real heartfelt care? He is surely then the dispassionate One whose 'love' is clinical, aloof from our concerns. What empathy can he feel when I go through the minor or major grief that life on earth brings, if he is safely closeted away in heaven, surrounded by the eternal luxury of angelic lullabies, comforted by day-in-day-out adulation? What kind of friendship can I form with such a God?

Nicholas P. Wolterstorff, Professor of Philosophical Theology at Yale Divinity School, says he had seriously to reconsider his theology after the death of his own son. Shattered by grief, Wolterstorff concluded that God could not possibly be unmoved by human tragedy. 'I found that picture of God as blissfully unperturbed by this world's anguish impossible to accept – *existentially* impossible. I could not live with it; I found it grotesque.'[5]

Genesis clearly tells us that we are made in the image of God – and surely that has to include our emotions.

Every parent has probably experienced one of those 'Mummy/Daddy – watch me!' moments when a child triumphantly learns a new skill – riding a bike unaided, swimming their first width of the pool, writing their name for the very time in those huge, delightful letters.

---

[4] Jürgen Moltmann, adapted from *The Crucified God* (Harper & Row, 1974)

[5] 'Does God Suffer?' *Modern Reformation* (Sept-Oct 1999), p45

The child longs for their parent to show enthusiastic interest and encouragement in that moment of development. Is our God any the less interested? I affirm that he is interested, and watches our progress and pain with passion, and not detachment.

When I first became a Christian, a church I visited regularly had a huge, gothic inscription above the pulpit: the King James English now seems quaint, but every time I went there I felt that the words of the preacher were

HE CARETH
FOR YOU

wonderfully buttressed by the truth of that biblical text emblazoned in fading gold paint: 'He careth for you.'[6]

Surely he does care, particularly as we struggle across life's battlefields. He cares when we hit those heady moments of temptation, when you and I are standing at the cross-roads of moral chaos if we make the wrong choice. Heaven is on tiptoe, with God's angelic friends willing me to choose holiness and godliness, yelling their support from that stadium on high, the loudest roar of encouragement emanating from the throne of God himself, as the Father cheers me on.

Surely, the biblical injunction that you and I should not 'grieve' him suggests that clearly we can bring him grief? And when tragedy visits me, two and two seems to equals five, and life just doesn't add up, I pray and ask for grace from One whose heart is really stirred about my loss. Passion means that God has invited me into a measure of partnership and participation with him – and that my prayers, desires and opinions count.

---

[6] 1 Peter 5:7

How can he love me and be indifferent to my thoughts and views – fallen and incomplete though they are? I recently saw a catchy little Christian slogan that filled me with horror: 'If you want to hear God laugh, then tell him your plans.' Such a God would be a mocking despot, amused at the plight of humanity, in the same way that we might grin at the relentless journey into nowhere that a caged hamster takes on its wheel. We laugh, but then again we put the hamster in the cage, and the wheel in there with him too. Is God similarly amused at our hapless plight? He does not dismiss my opinions, hope and dreams with a couldn't-care-less sweep of the divine hand. If that were the case, prayer would be meaningless.

And our own personalities will be affected by our understanding of God as either passionate or apathetic. I have met too many Christians who have an inherent suspicion of expressed emotion (dismissing all such expression as *emotionalism*, which is something quite different, and involves hysteria, pretence, and manipulation). Some of them are quick to condemn any emotion as being suspect at best and deception at worst. Their perception of God is simply a mirror of themselves; their Lord is calmly unmoved by anything, and they want to be like him.

Passionate – yet consistent and faithful

God agonised over Israel, and suffered with her suffering: Hosea prophesied about a God whose heart 'churned within him' over his people, who 'provoked' and 'grieved' him. Like a spurned lover, God was a husband who Israel cuckolded like a whore, he was like a compassionate mother moved for her children, and then was depicted as the ecstatic father of a wayward son, the party planner welcoming the returning sinner. At various times in the Bible, he is said to be grieved, angry, pleased, joyful and moved by pity. Expressing profound joy, God sings and claps his hands as he delights in his children.

GOD SINGS AND CLAPS HIS HANDS AS HE DELIGHTS IN HIS CHILDREN

Some suggest that these biblical examples are only figures of speech[7] used to help us finite humans to understand the infinite God. But even if that were true, the images of passion that are employed are utterly misleading if the true God is without passion. Our actions matter, our tears are shared. At times when our landscape is bleak, we remember that we will never be totally alone again. There really is One who can say, 'I know how you feel.'

Passion fuels a desire to give pleasure. Joys are in preparation, and future delightful moments are currently in the process of his architectural design and construction. In one of my better husbandly moments, I diligently planned that Kay would receive a gift from me on each of the twenty-one days of a trip that took me overseas. It took quite a while to hide all of the presents around the house, and then figure out ways for her to find the clue each

---

[7] Anthropopathisms – figurative expressions ascribing human passions to God. Just as we know that God does not really have hands, feet or eyes, but yet the Bible uses such terms to describe him – anthropomorphisms.

morning that would lead her to a different spot and a new surprise. Without reducing God to the level of a heavenly Santa, my experience of him has definitely been that his passion means that he delights in being the Father who prepares and gives extravagantly good gifts: the delightful late night glass of wine and easy laughter shared with beloved friends: the breathtaking vista of the Colorado mountains; the whispered 'I love you' from a son or daughter; and the material provision that is our daily bread. Of course, this latter truth can be twisted into a warped, self-centred 'prosperity gospel' – which again strips God's giving of grace. He showers us with kindness, not because our slavish adherence to certain cosmic principles enables us to manipulate the divine vending machine into giving us what we want, but rather because he greatly loves us. Dallas Willard remarks that God is 'always at play throughout the earth.' My experience is that often, bizarrely, he has me in mind when he is at creative play.

ᕲ ᕰ

EVEN THE WRATH OF GOD IS PART OF THAT PASSIONATE LOVE

ᕲ ᕰ

Those who are passionate about others are loyal to them when everyone else flees as deserters; they defend when all others go on the attack. The passionate have eyes open to see good where no one else sees it. And the passionate push through disappointment and hurt. Surely our God has been this to us – we have hurt him too many times but he keeps coming back, faithful One that he is.

Even the wrath of God is part of that passionate love – it is the fruit of intense care, albeit frustrated care. God's anger, as T. S. Eliot once said, is 'the unfamiliar Name' for his love. He is sometimes angry, because love and care cannot be indifferent. In that sense, grace begets anger. God's heart towards humanity is neither cool nor apathetic; again, the cross reveals to us a sense of the desperation of love. Nothing is held back by the Father and the Son as they pursue a wayward world with relentless urgency. The passion of God for us in that sense is a 'wild' love. A passionate God? Surely he is.

GOD THEREFORE CHOOSES TO ENTER INTO OUR PAIN

But let's not stray into the idea of a God *dominated* by passion, overwhelmed by it all. Those who struggle with the idea of God being passionate rightly react, I believe, against the notion that God is therefore the unwitting victim of whatever pain humans might cause him – as one 'classic theist' writes, 'that places God in the hands of angry sinners.'

Passion can infer a lack of control, or an untamed reaction to provocation – hence the term 'crimes of passion.' But God is never out of control, flying off the handle, or subject to mood swings or emotional power surges.

'The God of the Bible is much *more* emotional than we are, not less so!' Someone else sarcastically replied, 'Really? Does your god have even bigger mood swings than my mother-in-law?' The point was clear, even if made indelicately. It is a serious mistake to impute any kind of thoughts to God that are cast in the same mould as human passions—as if God possessed a temper subject to involuntary oscillation...[8]

---

[8] 'God without mood swings – recovering the doctrine of divine impassibility' – Philip R Johnson, excerpted from Douglas Wilson (Ed.), *Bound only once*, (Canon Press, 2001)

Perhaps we could say that God therefore chooses to enter into our pain – he deliberately chooses to be moved by us – a solid grace, if you will. My heart can be stirred by a well selected musical chord change, my tears sometimes flow because I am exhausted more than deeply moved. But the passion of God for you is that which he has purposely decided to embrace.

I hear God weeping

It was a small group – the Council of Management of Spring Harvest – that had gathered for a couple of days of retreat and prayer for the Main Event. Our time had certainly included stimulating dialogue and discussion, but now it was time to stop talking. We waited for a while in prayer, doing that which we Christian activists often find so very difficult – being silent. Suddenly, the quietness in my head was punctuated by a sound which seemed uncanny, unearthly – and the phrase began to form in my consciousness:

'I can hear God weeping.'

Moments like this fill me with dread: having navigated my way through a fair amount of charismatic wishful thinking, and prophesies that really weren't, it therefore increases my stress levels to the red zone when faced with the possibility that God may be speaking to me – and that I might have to share that with others. And I need to say that in writing this now, I have no more right to be believed than the worship leader who said 'nothing has changed in heaven' – but as I weighed *his* words, I invite you to weigh mine. God seemed to be expressing just how very much he does care about people, particularly his people, who been blinded to beautiful grace: he cries for them.

Passionate about me

The actress Sally Field was ruthlessly pilloried as a result of her now infamous Oscar acceptance speech in 1984. Field, who won the Best Actress award for *Places in the Heart*, gushed, 'I can't deny the fact you like me. Right now, you like me!' But what sounded like an overspill of narcissism was perhaps more likely the result of genuine heartfelt surprise from Field that she was the one chosen for such an honour.

Perhaps most of us – except those either incredibly secure or blinded by conceit – feel rather bemused, if not shocked, that we are liked and loved by others. We are grateful for their love, but we know all too well the treacherous inner space that is *us*, that private enclave that sometimes shames us. We are all too painfully conscious of that internal cauldron of mixed motives, petty jealousies, lusts and selfishness. We are probably grateful that, apart from untimely slippages of character that reveal what's inside us, we can keep it all hidden from view. Still, knowing ourselves as we do, the revelation that we are liked and loved can still be quite a shock.

But of course, there is One who knows his way around that inner us far more proficiently than we do: God himself, who is familiar with all that stuff that could make us crimson faced in seconds. And yet, in that knowing, he insists on telling us that we are his beloved, that we are the proverbial apples of his eye, the objects of his passion. It is surely easier to believe in a God who generically loves the *world* rather than an all-knowing suitor who specifically loves *me*. Yet this is grace: the knowledge and experience of being loved, accepted and cared for by the beautiful, energetic and passionate God: One who has opened his heart to me, enabling me to bring a smile to his face or a tear to his eye in turn.

Of course, he will have his own day at his own Oscars. Scripture reveals a God who anticipates meeting his faithful with the most timeless and eternal reward: 'Well done, good and faithful servants.' Perhaps even then, such a tangible experience of tender grace and passion will ignite our exclamation, delivered to the passionate God: 'you like me; right now, you like me...' Grace invites us to choose to believe it.

3

I WILL EMBRACE THE HOPE THAT I CAN CHANGE AND GROW

Now, with God's help, I shall become myself.
Soren Kierkegaard

The single belief most toxic to a relationship is the belief that the other person cannot change.
Psychologist Aaron Beck

Forever the same

My name is Jeff, and I am tired.

At least that's how I would introduce myself if I was sitting in one of those support groups where you go around the circle, sharing your name and most pressing problem, as per *Alcoholics Anonymous*. These days, 'I'm tired' tumbles out of my mouth almost automatically, mainly because I usually am. Commuting across the Atlantic Ocean once every three weeks may sound like a glamorous way to live: and yes, I am grateful for the changing scenery that travel brings. But being cooped up in a silver tube surrounded by three hundred fellow fighters against flatulence is not glamorous at all; on the contrary, particularly when we play 'name that food' at mealtimes. I live in Colorado, and spend a huge amount of time in Britain, which runs its national life seven hours ahead of the folks in the Rocky Mountains. This time zone shift means that I often find myself

preaching at 10am, with a body that is wearily inform-
ing me that it's really 3am, and preaching – and indeed
anything – shouldn't be done then, it not being natural.
Thus the instant affirmation often given whenever I'm
asked how I am: 'I'm fine, thank you, but tired.'

Recently, Kay and I enjoyed a holiday with friends in
the Canary Islands – which I would recommend, despite
the presence of lots of British grandmothers who sported too many tattoos and too few clothes. I came back
from the balmy week refreshed, renewed and, if I may
say this without sounding like an efficient cleaning
product, full of zest. Bumping into a colleague at the
office, I was asked, 'How are you?' – and my response
was delivered without thought, the usual mechanical
mantra; 'Fine, but tired.' Then it hit me. *I'm not tired at
all. I feel great. I've been on holiday.* I quickly tried to correct myself, and affirm that I was indeed feeling rested
and relaxed: but it was too late. They were already
responding: 'Yes, you do look a bit weary'…

Mine is surely a trivial example, but it is a parable of
how many of us live: we have decided what we are, and
what we probably will be, and don't think much about
our ever being different to any significant degree. We
have come to know our strengths and weaknesses, and
after a brief but jolly sprint in the heady, early days of
our being Christians, in terms of personal growth, some
of us have now slowed down to a meandering walk – or
maybe ground to a complete standstill. This is what I
am, nothing's going to change now. Of course, such a
life is utterly boring. One Christian writer describes the
second coming of Jesus as 'the next exciting event on
God's calendar.' His assertion makes 'the meantime'

look very tedious indeed: the possibility that something gripping or interesting might happen – for God or us – between now and the apocalypse seems remote. Thus some take heart from the biblical words, 'we shall all be changed' but see that change as limited to the other side of eternity. Not much is anticipated this side of the second coming or death. Carry on regardless, with more of the same.

Such resignation reminds me of a childhood hero: Popeye the Sailorman. Turbo-charged by a squeezed tin of spinach, and blessed

WE SHALL ALL BE CHANGED

with arm muscles the size of grapefruits, Popeye could make mincemeat out of his bearded rival Brutus any day. I couldn't quite figure out what he saw in the impossibly thin Olive Oyl (who would probably be banned these days because she might inspire anorexia) but I loved the gnarled old salt anyway. Yet all was not quite well with my sailor friend who clenched a pipe permanently between his teeth, as John Ortberg has noted in *The Life you've always wanted*.[1] You see, Popeye was fond of singing a hopeless song, *I yam what I yam*. His was such a sad lament, as he surrendered himself to the sentence of never being able to be anything more than he was: change for Popeye was completely out of the question.

Contrast the sailorman's song with the story of Jean Valjean in Victor Hugo's *Les Miserables*. In Hugo's classic, Valjean was a thief who was transformed by grace and kindness. A prisoner on parole, yet branded by his past and his prison number, Valjean is given food and shelter

---

[1] John Ortberg, *The Life you've always wanted*, (Zondervan, 2003)

by a kindly clergyman, but spits on the generous hospitality he has enjoyed by stealing some valuable silverware from the priest's home. Caught red-handed by the gendarme, he is stunned to hear the priest tell the police officer to release him, insisting that the stolen candelabras were a gift, and giving Valjean some more items which, says the priest, 'he had forgotten.' Valjean is overwhelmed by grace upon grace, and his life's direction is dramatically altered by that moment. Grace has changed him for ever, and the metamorphosis continues through the rest of his days. Finally he dies a good and godly man, beloved and serenaded by his adopted daughter and her husband, and summoned into the presence of God by a shimmering white angel. Not only has he vacated the prison gang, but he has also been set free from the cellblock of sameness – and all by the power of grace experienced, in this case, through human kindness and generosity. The musical version of *Les Miserables* is a personal favourite of mine: I've been to four performances. The songs are haunting – and *I yam what I yam* is not among them.

GRACE OFFERS
US FREEDOM

Help *is* available

Most of us look for help from an external source when we are trying to alter a significant pattern of behaviour: we bounce around in front of our *You too can have buttocks of steel* exercise videos, or try to escape nicotine cravings by chewing gum that tastes of old cigarettes.

We get a patch, a personal trainer, a support group, or a resolution for December 31st. Some of these 'helps' are really useful, and some of them are less so: as the new year bells chime midnight and we cheer, we hope upon hope that this will indeed be the year when things – and more than things, we ourselves – actually will be different. Without sounding too jaundiced, let's face it: our calendar centred aspirations are tinged with illogical optimism. But there are more solid and trustworthy resources to hand; grace provides us with something far more than wishful thinking.

The fact of there being a God means that we *can* grow and change. A universe without a God should indeed be filled with static people who have 'owned their story' and are now content to be nothing other than what they are. But everything is different if there is a helping God who has grace ready to work within us: power for change. Grace grabs and shakes us and yells, 'You can really be different!'

We have already touched on the truth that God is beautiful – yet he is one who wishes to share and indeed transfuse his beauty to others, creating a family likeness through grace. So Scripture calls us to a life, not only of morality, but of God-likeness – or perhaps Christ-likeness is a term that we would feel more comfortable with. Grace is not just about the transformation of our ideas – but rather the changing of us, through the life of God at work within us daily.

Grace offers us freedom. 'It is for freedom that Christ has set us free.'[2] Tragically, the idea of freedom has been

---

[2] Galatians 5:1

twisted to suggest that true liberation comes from simply being allowed to be what we are; but the God of destiny and purpose offers us freedom entwined in his purposes, the opportunity to become mature, developed human beings – the freedom to become. Our tomorrows no longer need to be dictated by old patterns of behaviour: through Jesus, the prison gates of sin, shame and self are flung wide open. Grace calls us out of those jailhouses towards new, more hopeful horizons, as we are gradually developed and shaped by grace. God the beautiful is totally committed to accepting us as we are: and equally committed to transforming us, by ongoing acts of transfusing beauty. He's been in the change business for a long time.

You too can have a body like mine

We've all seen those 'before and after' advertisements: those who want us to diet, or get more muscle by using the latest body building gadgets, or even submit ourselves to the plastic surgeon's scalpel usually employ a common marketing strategy. We are shown a photograph of the sad overweight chap, and next to it we have a grinning, chiselled hunk – the leaner version of the old man and all because of this stunning milkshake that surely tastes like wild berries. The photographs are visual credentials. They let us know: this stuff really works.

Biblical history is also a photograph gallery of sorts, a collection of 'before' and 'after' stories, all of which are included to tell us that, in a sense, we too can have a body like *them*. A trembling whiner like Gideon is changed into a wild warrior, who casts fear and caution aside and routs the hated Midianites. Impetuous Peter, who cruised around for much of his life with mouth in fourth gear and brain in neutral, becomes the bold spokesperson for the eleven, healing power coursing through his shadow. Hannah, rejected by the religious elite as a mumbling old soak, mothers the mighty Samuel. A naïve shepherd boy knocks a giant over and becomes a king. As we open our Bibles, over and over again God shows us that his grace has been the agent for revolutionary change in the lives of a motley assortment of rogues, doubters and accomplished sinners: but this is more than mildly fascinating historical data: their God is our God. He changed them – and he can change us.

ENTWINED IN HIS PURPOSES

Of course, such change is gradual, which is frustrating. I really want a diet that takes off the extra pounds today, or a work-out programme that will give me a washboard flat stomach, by, shall we say, Friday? Trudging through the next year of disciplined choices and denying myself ice cream is a trek I'd rather avoid. That desire for quick, easy change is sometimes reflected in the Christian culture. At the end of a stirring service, we are invited to go forward for prayer, to receive the blessing/healing/breakthrough/answer/touch *right now*, a kind of Nescafe spirituality. While God does surely act in epic moments, much of his work spans months and years. And we must know that this is the truth, lest we lose hope. Sometimes despair descends on us when we get impatient with our own seeming lack of development and growth. But when God is at work, transformation is a lifelong journey, not a quick fix.

Some biographies of famous Christians tend to gloss over their faults; but we need to remember that all of God's greatest heroes were flawed, in-the-process human beings. Martin Luther, C. S. Lewis, and Lord Shaftesbury all serve as examples of 'flawed greatness' – heroes enrolled in the lifelong school of grace – and not all of their flaws were ironed out. They died as people still in the change process.

> WHEN GOD IS AT WORK, TRANSFORMATION IS A LIFELONG JOURNEY, NOT A QUICK FIX

Martin Luther swore terribly, had an obsession with bowel movements, and, tragically, was intemperate in his words about Jews – and was quoted by the architects of the Nazi holocaust as a result. C.S. Lewis admitted (in letters to a long-term Belfast friend) that he had some problems with his sexuality, with some tendencies towards sado-masochism. Lord Shaftesbury was a much celebrated evangelical reformer; when his funeral procession travelled from his home in Grosvenor Square to Westminster Abbey, the streets were lined with representatives from the many organisations that he had served. They held banners that said 'I was naked and you clothed me.' Even the poorest wore some token of mourning. Yet he was, by his own admission, 'a mass of contradictions.' He tended to alienate his friends by his habit of making insignificant matters seem more important than they were, and crusading about incidentals; he criticised the work of the Salvation Army, and was infamous for his misplaced intolerance of others' viewpoints. And he was sometimes resented by the poor for his insistence that he really knew what was best for them. None of the above is written to encourage us in sin, but to affirm us in the process of transformation; God uses the flawed, and changes us gradually as we submit to him. But if that is to happen, we must not only submit to his actions – the passive 'let go and let God' idea that did the rounds a few years ago. Once again we note that grace calls us to be intentional people, who make good, thoughtful choices.

Turning off cruise control

My car is fitted with a truly beautiful invention – the wonder of cruise control. Eager to save my right foot from cramping, the designers came up with a button that I can press when I'm on the motorway, the road is relatively clear, and fluctuations in speed seem unlikely. I can decide that I plan to proceed at 69.999 miles per hour, press the magic button, and no further pressure on the accelerator is required of me. My car will cruise at that speed until I tell it otherwise; wonderful.

Sadly, it's all too easy to switch to cruise as a Christian. It takes no effort at all to turn off my brain and drift along, never thinking through carefully the consequences of my actions. I am lulled into thinking that, if I am a person of 'sound character', then I will usually do the right thing. I have come to believe that there is no such thing as a person of sound character. You and I may do the right thing today and make an utterly immoral choice tomorrow: such things are not set. Obviously, goodness is something of a habit, so a positive history is a good indicator that we are more likely to do the right thing, but there are no guarantees. Growth comes as a result of a million good choices – all prompted and empowered by grace, yet our choices still.

Moment by moment decisions aren't easy when you're on 'cruise'. Temptation usually invites us to switch off our brains, suspend our critical faculties and forget – or deny – all the wisdom we've gained through the years, and plunge into a moment of utter madness. Temptation is an invitation to us to become irrational people, who shove aside all judgement about the consequences of our actions, so that we can just fulfil an urge. And in this battle – and war it surely is – we aren't helped by our relativist culture, where the word 'sin' seems to belong only in the vocabularies of intolerant prudes who need to get out more: sad folks who are probably trying to wreck everyone else's fun because they aren't having much themselves. The result of all of this is that growth, change and maturity are stymied, as we come up the roadblock that is sin. Many of us stay halted at that boring junction for years, or even a lifetime.

Whatever happened to sin?

Prior to 1975, many dictionaries did not even contain the word *judgemental*. Now, the word is very much in common usage, in a culture where, as one journalist says,

'Judging evil is widely considered worse than doing evil.' Utter tolerance is the new mantra: perhaps the only thing our culture won't tolerate is intolerance! Encouraging a woman to embark on a disastrous adulterous affair, a character in the film *Unfaithful* declares, 'There's no such thing as good or bad. Just choices.' To call anything sin is unfashionable.

MTV broadcast a programme that looked at modern attitudes to the traditional 'Seven deadly sins'. VJ Kurt Loder, who narrated the broadcast, commented: 'There's a vague sense that sin, if it exists, is surely a problem of psychology. The seven deadly sins are not evil acts, but, rather, universal human compulsions that can be troubling and highly enjoyable.' Does anyone stop to analyse what kind of world we would share if Loder was correct in this conclusion – where the use of child pornography is no longer evil – where genocide is an economic and political option, and drug trafficking just meets a need?

GROWTH COMES AS A RESULT OF A MILLION GOOD CHOICES

During the recent heated debates about the proposed ordination of an openly gay priest as bishop, a Vice Chancellor at a leading British University used the graduating ceremony to attack those who felt that this proposal was immoral and unbiblical. The Vice-Chancellor regretted that, 'We now have a national church which is more concerned about what bishops do with their private parts than their brains' – implying that intellectual ability is more significant and important than moral consistency.

We are…uncomfortable with guilt. Listen to people discuss guilt in general, and one message comes through with conviction: guilt is bad. But it's those who feel no guilt who are most dangerous – the psychopathic liars and killers … and the hate mongers of the world who feel totally justified in their ghastly acts. In August 1968, a small cult under the hypnotic direction of Charles Manson brutally slaughtered seven people in what became known as the Tate-LaBianca murders. At his trial, after the court found him guilty, Manson was asked if he had any comments before the judge handed down his sentence. Wild-eyed and scraggly, Manson stood, pointed to the jury, and seethed, 'You have no right to try me! I did what I felt was right.'[3]

And we Christians can easily get lost in this amoral fog. In a recent leaders' gathering, my friend Joel Edwards spoke of his conversion experience, when he had a great awareness and conviction of sin. Joel challenged the meeting with the question – whatever has happened to sin these days?

The awareness of sin used to be our shadow. Christians hated sin, feared it, fled from it, grieved over it. Some of our grandparents agonised over their sins. A man who lost his temper might wonder whether he could still go to Holy Communion … in today's group confessionals it is harder to tell. The newer language of Zion fudges: 'Let us confess our problem with human relationship adjustment dynamics, and especially our feebleness in networking.' Or, 'I'd just to share that we need to target holiness as a growth area.' Where sin is concerned, people just mumble now…[4]

[3] Chris Blake, *Searching for a God to love*, (W Publishing, 2000)

[4] Cornelius Plantinga, *Not the way it's supposed to be: a breviary of sin*, (Grand Rapids, Wm B Eerdmans, 1995)

Legalistic ranting – producing unbiblical lists of things deemed right and wrong – is dangerous, manipulative, and produces immature people who can't think for themselves. But mumbling about sin won't help any of us towards growth either. The fact is that grace can be, and is, abused. The message of grace is both dynamic and dangerous in that we can use it as a licence to sin; Christian leaders are constantly facing pastoral dilemmas with people who decide to do something that they know is clearly wrong, on the basis that forgiveness will be available once the deed is done. This is no new dilemma: Paul

> GRACE LEADS US OUT FROM SLAVERY

faced it and dealt with it convincingly in his epistle to the Romans. Grace leads us out from slavery to sin, but into a relationship that is likened to being a bond-slave both to Christ and to righteousness (Rom. 6:16, 18, 19, 1 Cor. 7:22). Those who use grace as a permit-to-sin have failed really to understand its true character. Grace calls us to radical obedience. Ted Koppel is correct in his wry observation: 'What Moses brought down from Mount Sinai were not the Ten Suggestions.'

Other disasters await the church that refuses to confront sin prophetically: history shows us that such a church will increasingly mirror the culture in its values and lifestyle. Mission will be ineffective – because a culture that has no awareness of sin will surely be indifferent to the gospel, seeing it as 'medicine' that it doesn't need, a cure for a sickness that it doesn't know it has. The good news is not good unless there is some awareness that there is some bad news – that sin separates us from a holy God, taught by John the Baptist, Peter, Paul, and of course, Jesus, in his call to repentance. Grace only makes sense when we understand that grace is needed. Freedom will be an idea rather than a reality; instead of facing up to our chains, we call them by a different name. Ultimately, we end up being mastered by that which we refuse even to acknowl-

⮹ ⮸

GRACE ONLY MAKES
SENSE WHEN WE
UNDERSTAND THAT
GRACE IS NEEDED

⮹ ⮸

edge. Sin is not a neutral force: there is no level ground when we are in its embrace, only a pathway of gradual deterioration in our character and of increasing domination and oppression from the control of sin itself: it seeks to 'have us' or 'master us'.

Sin has the effect of gradually 'hardening our hearts', desensitising us to any sense of moral failure – thus sin begets sin. If we are ever to grow, we need to awaken from our moral comas: and here again God's grace comes to help us, albeit in what is sometimes an unwelcome way. In his book, *Pain – the gift nobody wants,* the late Dr. Paul Brand wrote about his work with people with leprosy, who are unable to feel any pain in their extremities. Because they do not have the 'gift' of the danger signal that is pain, they continuously injure themselves, and lose their fingers and their toes. Pain speaks for our benefit, as an unwelcome but vital indicator that something is wrong. Conviction – that experience when our moral sensitivities are aroused and we know that we are in the wrong, and that repentance is required – can serve the same purpose, guiding us away from sin and its consequences. The ability to feel conviction is not only a normative biblical experience, but is an experience of grace. Conviction is not a miserly swipe from a kill-joy God, but a call from a loving Father away from that which will hurt us, damage those around us, and ultimately, could destroy our world.

The ability to feel guilt pangs is a hint from heaven that we are more than animals: it is a sign of nobility. The Holy Spirit shows us our sin, not because we are worthless, but because God sees us, by his grace, as being so worthwhile. Conviction shows us that our sinful behaviour is incompatible with our dignity as children of God. Under conviction, we see that we have stooped down to sin; but we receive an instant invitation to step up out of the mire and the muck of the pigpen and back into the warmth of the Father's house again.

Conviction is God's grace calling us to take a specific, reachable step, hand in hand with him, like a child skipping stone-by-stone across a river, not a daunting call to jump across the awesome cauldron of the Niagara Falls. Conviction is surely a great grace gift, and a vital component in a life of growth and change.

A youthful dip

Last week I watched as thirty-seven people were baptised in water. Our church is one of the you're-not-really-dunked-unless-you're-drenched kinds, so there was a lot of nervous splashing, a fair bit of joyful spluttering as water rushed up nostrils, and some tearfully poignant moments as epic grace stories were shared.

The experience made me recall the night that I was baptised in water, some thirty years ago now. That distant Sunday evening is burned deep into my memory for a number of reasons, some of which are *very* embarrassing and cause me to blush even now as I remember them. Our church had the tradition that everyone would share a brief 'testimony' before being immersed – and then the whole congregation would sing a verse of a song as the candidate came up out of the water. It was a simple, moving ceremony – which I messed up by trying to bring a little 'creative' variation to the evening. Tragically, I came up with the bright idea of turning my testimony into a song, which I would sing (and accompany myself on the guitar) as a duet with a friend before going down into the baptismal tank. You can perhaps imagine just how hideous this was. The words and tune are long lost now – and if anyone has a recording of the evening, I will surely have to kill them. But I remember enough: my friend was singing in the key of 'G', and I think I was warbling in the key of 'H'. But the church just smiled, their eyes shining as these two new Christians made a joyful 'noise' (more noise than joy). They even applauded when we finished – though that was probably because they were so relieved that our performance was over.

The second problem came when I was actually being baptised. For some reason I kicked my legs up when I went under the water, as if trying to score an overhead goal – and drenched the first three rows of people in the congregation. I emerged seconds later, thrilled, delighted, and baptised into God's family – some of whom were very wet indeed. Yet still they smiled, and applauded again, even if some of the older ladies sitting near the front looked like blue rinsed drowned rats.

But, even with my awful singing and widespread soaking, it was a night of real celebration. I gratefully remember all the hugs and the handshakes and the genuine sense of elation that was mine as I realised that I belonged to this new family, a family that will last forever.

I AM MORE AT
PEACE WITH
MYSTERY

But most of all, I recall the total sense of devotion to Jesus that I felt. It was captured by the little chorus that the congregation sang as I came up out of the tank.

'Follow, follow, I will follow Jesus, anywhere, everywhere I will follow on.'

How easy it was to join in with that song. I was only seventeen years old, and it all seemed so straightforward to profess that I was going to be with Jesus all the way, whatever the cost. My faith was headily enthusiastic, naively passionate, and quite dangerously simplistic in some areas. Our minister was an excellent teacher and preacher, but I had not been around long enough to have accumulated much depth or wisdom from his words, and so my faith was buttressed by too many slogans, clichés and easy answers. It was certainly real, but not terribly thought through. And I was also at the age where one still wants to be a rock star today, a millionaire business person tomorrow, and something quite different this time next week. Just months before my conversion I had decided to become a Communist – and that lasted for a good month or so. I became a Christian and professed lifelong allegiance during what was obviously the adolescent season of uncertainty.

The last three decades have shaped me into a very different person from the one that took a youthful dip. I, like most of us, have seen my fair share of nauseating church politics, hypocrisies and dull-your-faith disappointments. And I have realised that the simple answers that I clutched with confidence back then just won't work. I've become more of an agnostic in some areas – and am more at peace with mystery. Youth made me feel I had all the answers – and the years have helped me realise that I don't need to have them. All of which has made me see that, although my profession of faith then was genuine and authentic, yet the person that I am now has consciously to decide to follow Jesus. Life has produced a revised me: and that me doesn't need to be born again, again: but I need to determine that with my contemporary temptations and potential distractions, I still want to sing that powerful song: Today, I want to offer the person that I have become to Jesus, so that I can continue to become all that he calls me to be:

'Anywhere, everywhere, I will follow on.'

My name is Jeff, and I want to grow.

4

I WILL REFUSE TO ARGUE WITH GOD'S GRACIOUS FORGIVENESS

We read, we hear, we believe a good theology of grace. But that's not the way we live. The good news of the Gospel of grace has not penetrated the level of our emotions.
David Seamands, Counsellor

Most Christians have enough religion to feel guilty about their sins, but not enough to enjoy life in spirit.
Martin Luther

Arguing with God

I've never met an angel face to face, but if I did, we'd probably have a fight.

I'm not proud of that admission, and have found myself somewhat envious of those who claim to have bumped into one of God's winged warriors. While some of those stories may need to be taken with the proverbial pinch of salt, and filed away with the 'I was abducted by aliens and had one of their children in a hospital on Jupiter' ruses, nevertheless, it must be stunning to be on the receiving end of an angelic visit. Still, I reckon that my first reaction would be fear (of the bloodcurdling screaming kind) and then the wrestling match would begin. After all, fights of a sort usually break out when angels touch down on earth: perhaps that's why they seem to begin most encounters with humans by saying 'peace': could it be they are hoping for an incident free and indeed quiet visit?

So why do I have this expectation of conflict in the event that I might bump into a passing seraphim? It's based on the track record that I find in Scripture. When I study the biblical moments when angels appear, they seem to follow a consistent pattern that goes something like this:

An angel of the Lord appears. Some ignition of fear is noted in the heart of the human being visited, ranging from dumbstruck awe to full blown terror. The angel immediately begins to announce some good, or at very least, very *unusual* news (I qualify this as, for example, the announcement of pregnancy to a teenage virgin was indeed good news for humanity, but hardly easy news for her to take, living as she did in the culture where people who had slept together outside of marriage could risk starring at a stoning). When this good news begins to sink in, the fight then begins in earnest: mainly because the news is simply just *too* good for the tiny human heart and brain to take.

Gideon argued with the idea that he could be Israel's next field marshal, because he felt so insignificant and weak, and with good reason: the encounter with the angel took place when he was a fearful fugitive hiding in a winepress. Sarah just about fell over laughing at the thought of rekindled romance – and a child as a result, with her wizened old Abraham. The news was so outrageous, it was simply...laughable.

Zechariah was dumbstruck – quite literally – as a result of hearing that John the Baptist was on the way. In his little skirmish with Gabriel, he certainly came out the worst. This habit of wrestling with God, and struggling with his grace in particular, seems common in human dealings with him. The prodigal son wails, 'I'm not worthy' when his father decides to throw such a fabulous party: but the protest was apparently drowned as his face was buried in the arms in his father, so close and intense was the welcome home hug. Peter almost went on strike when Jesus insisted on washing his sweaty feet: and Peter had to learn a vital lesson, which we'd do well to note ourselves. When you're around the Son of God, you have to allow the Son of God to do what he does best; namely, clean you up. This is non-negotiable: yet Peter struggled, at least for a while. And there was another little skirmish later on in Peter's life. While he slept, he experienced a vision: a sheet loaded with very nasty un-kosher animals was lowered before him, and he was commanded by God to get up and eat. To our gentile ears, this sounds like no big deal. We should remember that this action was the cultural equivalent of God lowering a fully stocked bar into a Salvation Army Hall on Sunday morning, with a voice from heaven saying, 'tambourines and tubas down, please: everybody have a beer...' So called righteous indignation would break out, and an argument would surely begin. How often are we like Peter, who had to be told not to 'call unclean that which God called clean.' So often we do the very same thing: except we are calling ourselves unclean when God has a different verdict about us because of what Jesus has done.

> THIS HABIT OF WRESTLING WITH GOD... SEEMS COMMON IN HUMAN DEALINGS WITH HIM

Jonah was another fighter who raged at God – study the book named after him and you'll see he was quite incensed – and all because God insisted on being merciful to the hated Ninevites, the Nazi storm-troopers of the day. Jonah had parked himself in a front row seat outside the city in order to have a good view of the fire and brimstone that he hoped would rain on these pagans at any moment. When God decided to smile on them instead, Jonah was so overwhelmed with grief that he fervently prayed for death; the prophet of the Lord, his face a mask of rage, his fists bunched at heaven. Fights are frequent in the Bible – particularly in response to outrageous grace. It seems that we humans are prone to reverse the prayer of Jacob, who wrestled with God and yelled, 'I will not let you go until you bless me…' We are more likely to pray, 'I will not let you bless me, let me go.' The issue is sharply focused when we consider God's offer to forgive us. Simply put, we struggle and fight with his kindness; some us feeling unworthy of it (which is ironic – we *are* unworthy). For whatever reason, some of us seem to want to choose condemnation over freedom.

WE STRUGGLE AND FIGHT WITH HIS KINDNESS

Years after Abraham Lincoln had outlawed slavery in America, large members of the black population continued to live in slavery, either because they hadn't heard about the legal freedom that was theirs – or because they either chose slavery or felt unable to break free from it. Even after the great emancipation act of the cross, an area of continued slavery for many Christians is in the area of false guilt. Condemnation and shame all too often blight our lives and eclipse the light of grace.

Typically, shame overshadows us when:

• We have been raised on a constant emotional diet of being told that we are no good

• We are part of a local church that is more of a 'guilt machine' than a community of grace

• We have sinned in a specific area and have repented, but can't forgive ourselves or accept that we have been forgiven

• We have a faith that is dominated by subjective feelings rather than trust in what God says to us about our being forgiven in Scripture

Too many Christian live shame-driven lives. I wrote a book about this specific problem some years ago: *Walking Backwards: dealing with guilt*.[1] Permit me to use some of the material from that book here.

When we choose shame over grace, moments of 'spiritual high' are blighted by mental 'video replays' of our embarrassing and shameful history. And we begin to lose hope, because we are blinded to any of the steps of growth and change that I described in the last chapter. Even the most proficient can be unaware of any giftedness or progress in their lives if they are preoccupied with shame.

Whatever their accomplishments, they remain on the treadmill of failure. One committed Christian wrote of

[1] Jeff Lucas, *Walking backwards: dealing with guilt* (Scripture Union 1997), ISBN 0962019737

how she 'lugs around inside of me a dead weight of not-good-enoughness.' Catholic theologians describe people like this as the 'scrupulous' – they are forever guilty, and always confessing or making pledges and promises to God for fear that their current level of commitment does not satisfy him. Grace is there for them – but they feel unable to accept it.

Michelangelo Buonarroti (1475-1564) was one of the greatest artists of all time, a man whose name has become synonymous with the word 'masterpiece'. As an artist he was unmatched, the creator of works of sublime beauty that express the full breadth of the human condition.

But he was a socially inept, insecure man – the enmity between him and Leonardo da Vinci is famous. And he had episodes of crippling self doubt and crises of confidence in his own ability. During the painting of 'Creation Day' on the ceiling of the Sistine Chapel, he had a particularly difficult day up on the backbreaking scaffolding. That night the great man wrote these words in his journal:

'I am not a painter.' He was temporarily blinded to his own abilities.

John Quincy Adams (1767-1848) went through a similar myopic crisis, affirming that 'My life has been spent in vain and idle aspirations, and in ceaseless rejected prayers that something beneficial should be the result of my existence.'

Adams' 'vain and idle aspirations' led him to become an outstanding opponent of slavery, and Ambassador to Holland, Ambassador to Great Britain, Ambassador to Russia, Secretary of State, Senator, and President of the

United States. False guilt blinds us. It is an agonising fight. And for a few, it is literally a fight to the death.

John – not his real name – was a bright, popular guy who seemed to enjoy his work as an associate pastor in the church across town in the English Midlands. I never knew him that well, but he seemed to be intelligent and confident, enjoying life. But his smile masked an inner darkness. Prior to entering full time ministry, John had lived for a year or two in open rebellion towards God. He wasn't just immoral – he was per- versely immoral in his passion for

FALSE GUILT
BLINDS US

sexual deviancy. Then John came back to God. His repentance was total, his commitment unquestioned. But the sickening images of his past stained his soul. Try as he might, he couldn't forget the evil in his per- sonal history. He became convinced that he had blas- phemed the Holy Spirit, that he had bypassed the pos- sibility of forgiveness, even though his life and conduct clearly showed that the Holy Spirit was working over- time in his life and had been for years. My telephone screamed at 3am. It was John's minister. John had dis- appeared, leaving a note on his door: 'Burn my clothes, and consign my soul to hell.' He read in his Bible that some would be saved, but only by fire. He put his Bible down. He wrote his note. He went out into a lonely, windswept field, poured a can of petrol over his head and burned himself to death. This was no calm, mar- tyr's death – he breathed his last in agony. Perhaps John stepped over the threshold into mental illness; who knows what drives people when they find themselves in such deep personal despair? But, whatever the final diagnosis, one thing is sure: false guilt was his executioner. False guilt. Not something I should endure, perversely, for his Name's sake. Not just an incidental problem for the spiritually sensitive. False guilt – brutal murderer; John's killer.[2]

Why the big struggle?

Perhaps the fights start because God, the grace of God, really is so amazing, and usually leaves us with open mouths as a result. His generosity is staggering, and takes our breath away.

> Astonishment is precisely what is missing in so many of us in the church today. We have completed all the fill-in-the-blank Bible study workbooks and learnt all the Christian answers to questions about every conceivable topic ... the bottom line is this: if we are not astonished by Jesus, then we are following something other than the person described in the Bible.[3]

A number of episodes from the life of Jesus provide us with word-drawings that illustrate his superlative nature. When he provided breakfast for a team of worn out, frustrated fishermen, it's noted that a whole net full of teeming, silvery fish are on the menu. John seems to take delight in giving us the news of the fish count: 153.

The five thousand are fed, but of course there's more besides: twelve loaded baskets are left over after

---

[2] Adapted from *Walking Backwards*
[3] Craig Barnes, *Sacred Thirst*, (Zondervan, 2001)

everyone had their fill. Look beyond the miracle, and marvel at the generosity of that moment.

The Rabbis taught generosity of forgiveness, instructing the people to forgive one who offended them no less than three times. Jesus calls them to 'seventy times seven' forgiveness.

That wedding at Cana has always been hard to take, quite apart from the fact that Jesus chose to launch his ministry by providing the drinks for a party; not standard evangelical practice. A lady who tried to argue that teetotalism was a biblical requirement for all Christians (rather than that some would choose to abstain because of personal choice or conscience) sniffed when confronted with the Cana event. 'Yes, I know it's there, and I really wish he hadn't done that...'

THE GRACE OF GOD... LEAVES US WITH OPEN MOUTHS

And the greatest shock of all comes as we consider the cross. The sight of Christ hanging there is a scandal indeed, because it renders us helpless. If we could save ourselves, he would obviously not have trod that green hill far away. There God whips the mat of self sufficiency from beneath our feet, leaving only one place to stand – on grace ground.

Perhaps we struggle with grace because we have been taught to be uncomfortable with giving that we can't reciprocate. Adulthood has robbed us of the ability to receive. I think that children are usually more human than adults. They haven't been layered with societal add-ons like propriety and subtlety and tact and the tyranny of efficiency. Theirs is a season of play, wild imagining, discovery, giggling, and adventure: they haven't yet learned our stifling adult protocols. Children are often raw, unspoilt human beings, and so there is a freedom about them, a capacity for wonder that adulthood robs us of. We adults are so often uptight, emotionally constipated, and repressed: give a child a gift, and they receive it gladly. Indeed it has become vital that we educate our children not to 'take sweets from strangers' so trusting are they, and so willing to receive without protest or struggle. Give an adult a gift when there's no reasonable excuse – like a birthday or Christmas – and watch the fight begin. The same wrestling can so easily take place in our relationship with God. We have been taught not to receive. Developing suspicion is a sad part of our maturing.

Darkness is also at the heart of the struggle

The Bible makes clear the reality of a personal foe towards all Christians, in the person of Satan. The biblical description of Satan's character shows us that the favoured weapon in his arsenal is accusation – the relentless use of false guilt; he is even named in honour of the tactic – the word Satan means 'accuser'. Old Testament writers occasionally refer to their human enemies and accusers as 'satans'. The Psalmist refers five times to the human 'satans' that oppose him. Ever since his meteoric fall, Satan has 'sataned' – accused. Even God himself comes under attack from this relentless prosecutor. In the Eden dialogue, Satan accused God of being unreliable, and of having false, selfish motives. The deception was remarkably effective: remember, Eve had taken late afternoon walks in the garden with God – she was close friends with him. But still she was convinced by the smooth talking prosecutor who is also the father of lies. The one woman jury believed the persuasive speech. She ate, and snacked with Adam. Eyes opened, case

∾ ∾

WE HAVE BEEN
TAUGHT NOT TO
RECEIVE

∽ ∽

closed, paradise lost. Satan would like to recreate his courtroom triumph in Eden – in *our* minds. Even though Scripture shouts about God's amazing grace, endless mists of doubt still swirl around our subconscious. Like Eve, if we lose sight of the goodness of God, we will quickly lose the motivation to obey him. Satan is history's most prolific and gifted prosecutor. He has handled cases against Job, Joshua, and David. In the wilderness he came against the Lord Jesus. Through the wagging tongues of the Pharisees, he accused and blasphemed the Holy Spirit. If the Satanic attorney points the finger at everyone – even the great Judge himself – don't you think that he'll try to pull the same stunt on us?

Accusation is a wickedly clever strategy because it destroys faith for the present or hope for the future. If God hasn't forgiven me, then what is the point of anything? Suddenly a 'castle of thoughts' – a stronghold – is established in our thinking. Ed Silvoso defines strongholds thus: 'A stronghold is a mindset impregnated with hopelessness that causes us to accept as unchangeable situations that we know are contrary to the will of God.'

The feeling of being accused can be continuous. Scripture tags Satan as the one who accuses us 'day and night.' One writer describes Satan as 'the opposition party in God's parliament.' Consider the endless, droning voice of the politician who confronts and mocks everything that comes from the other side of house, and you've got a good picture of the accuser. Some Christians teach that a pressing thought that won't go away is probably from God. Unfortunately, Satan is happy to go on harassing and debating. And the tragedy is that the real authority – the Judge – has already delivered his verdict. Sadly, too many live heavy, burdened lives spoiled by shame:

> Shame is a very heavy feeling. It is a feeling that we do not measure up and maybe will never measure up to the sorts of people we are meant to be. The feeling, when we are conscious of it, gives us a vague disgust with ourselves, which in turn feels like a hunk of lead on our hearts.[4]

Shame ultimately drives us away from God, not towards him – with potentially disastrous personal and social consequences. Philosopher Friedrich Nietzsche, much quoted by Hitler and his Nazi regime, was the son of a Lutheran minister. Nietzsche developed a shame based view of God – a view that caused him to want to see the very idea of God destroyed; 'He saw with eyes that saw everything ... all my concealed disgrace and ugliness ... He crawled into my dirtiest nooks. This most curious one had to die.'

---

[4] Lewis Smedes

The dark strategy had worked well, with devastating results.

Compounding the confusion: the infallible conscience

One of the particular challenges that we face as Christians dealing with a sense of shame is that it is difficult to clarify what we are really feeling – and we do live in a Christian world that is very driven by the subjective. We are high on 'sensing' and 'feeling'

> SHAME ULTIMATELY DRIVES US AWAY FROM GOD

things – sometimes to our cost. Navigating our way through our inner landscape can be a daunting prospect: it's been said that 'feelings are mushy, difficult, non-palpable, slippery things … they are difficult to quantify, difficult to communicate, difficult even to distinguish within ourselves one from the other.' Intimidated, we do not even begin to sort out the tangle within – we just continue to 'feel' bad. In the last chapter we saw that *conviction* is a grace gift that leads us to change and growth: but *condemnation* and shame are confusing imitators of conviction.

Some Christians seem to treat their conscience as infallible: if we feel bad, then we must be bad. But this fails to recognise that the conscience can be damaged, seared, and falsely programmed. Culture and propaganda can even reprogramme our conscience to make good feel like evil – and evil feel good, as happened in Nazi Germany. There, propaganda used as a weapon to pervert the moral sense became a fine art. It soon seemed, for example, a positive duty to hate the Jews, and a good Nazi would doubtless have suffered *pangs of conscience* if he had been kind to one of the despised race.'[5] The exhortation that we should 'always let our conscience be our guide' is *not* a biblical injunction – it comes from the lips of Pinocchio's friend, Jiminy Cricket.

Some have oversensitive consciences – like Pauline, a Jehovah's Witness who came to Christ – and then threw all her Christmas cards out of the window because of a crisis of 'conscience' that had been programmed with Jehovah's Witness' teaching that Christmas was a season that the faithful should shun.

> To make conscience into God is a highly dangerous thing to do. For one thing ... conscience is by no means an infallible guide; and for another it is extremely unlikely that we shall ever be moved to worship, love, and serve a nagging inner voice that at worst spoils our pleasure and at best keeps us rather negatively on the path of virtue. Conscience can be so easily perverted or morbidly developed in the sensitive person, and so easily ignored and silenced by the insensitive, that it makes a very unsatisfactory God. For while it is probably true that every normal person has an embryo moral sense by which he can distinguish right and wrong, the development, non development, or perversion of that sense is largely a question of upbringing, training and propaganda...[6]

---

[5] Adapted from J B Phillips – *Your God is too small*, (London, Macmillan)

[6] J B Phillips, *Your God is too small*, (London: Macmillan), p15,16

Our conscience is a gift from God; but it needs careful tending and nurture to make sure that it doesn't excuse or cripple us.

Choosing freedom from false guilt

There are some for whom the issue of unresolved shame has brought them to a place where they need professional help and counselling. The following is not intended in any way as a simplistic solution to what can be deep psychological scars; but these steps are offered to help us to begin our exodus from shame.

- Realise that there is a strategy to rob you of grace: you are not abnormal or alone in these struggles – they are very common. We must not be ignorant about the tactics and schemes of the enemy (Eph. 6:11), as well as the general struggles that human beings have with grace and free gifts.

- Be clear about the issue – if you feel guilt because of current sin, then deal with that – do not try to reject genuine conviction by calling it shame.

- Recognise that our feelings are not the final arbiter of truth. Scripture is – and God's word about his willingness graciously to forgive is our final authority (1 Jn. 1:9). As Christians, we say that we believe in the inspiration of Scripture – why not accept and believe what God has to say about grace and forgiveness?

- Refuse to argue with God's verdict – when he pronounces us clean, then we must choose to rest in that decision.

Great sinners, greater Saviour

John Newton, who penned the hymn *Amazing Grace*, left school at the age of eleven to begin a life of debauchery and oppressing others as a mariner. Eventually he built a business as a slave trader, capturing West Africans and selling them as slaves to markets around the world. One day the grace of God put fear into Newton's heart, through a fierce storm. Terrified of a shipwreck, Newton began to read *The Imitation of Christ* by Thomas à Kempis. The book was used to lead him to a genuine conversion and a dramatic change in his way of life – eventually. For a while, Newton continued to sell slaves; in fact it took him some while to see that his profession wasn't consistent with being a Christian – and many Christians at that time supported slavery. Eventually, Newton not only saw the error of his ways, but also became a leading figure in the early years of the Evangelical movement, and he became a major player in the fight to end the slave trade, which was finally abolished in Britain in 1807, the year he died.[7] Feeling a definite call to study for ministry, Newton was encouraged and greatly influenced by John and Charles Wesley and George Whitefield. At

---

[7] Discussed in Steve Chalke, *He never said: Discovering the Real Message of Jesus*, (London: Hodder & Stoughton, 2000)

the age of 39, he became an ordained Anglican minister at the little village of Olney, near Cambridge. To add further impact to his powerful preaching, Newton introduced simple heart-felt hymns rather than the usual psalms in his services. When enough hymns could not be found, Newton began to write his own, often assisted by his close friend William Cowper. In 1779 their combined efforts produced the famous *Olney Hymns* hymnal. *Amazing Grace* was from that collection. He had plenty of shadows from his past that could have debilitated him completely, and left him overwhelmed by condemnation: but he chose to accept God's truly amazing pardon. Until the time of his death at the age of 82, John Newton never ceased to marvel at the grace of God that transformed him so completely.

I AM A GREAT SINNER: CHRIST IS A GREAT SAVIOUR!

Newton preached with loud enthusiasm shortly before his death 'My memory is nearly gone, but I remember two things: that I am a great sinner and that Christ is a great Saviour!'[8] He surely speaks for us all.

---

[8] Adapted from Kenneth W Osbeck, *Amazing Grace*, (Grand Rapids; Kregel Publishing, 1990)

5

I WILL OPEN MY EYES TO LOOK FOR GRACE

We have locked God into the so called sacred realms of church and healings and miracles and marvels … we seem to be trying so hard to 'bring down fire from heaven' in our worship services while all along God's favour is to be found in sunshine on our faces, the sea lapping at our toes, picking our children up at school, or a note from a caring friend.
Michael Frost

Many things occur between God and humanity which escape the attention of even those to whom they happen.
Rabbi Herschel

Grace is everywhere

P reaching – particularly as an itinerant who most weeks is a guest in yet another church somewhere – carries peculiar challenges, one of which is the moment in the service when someone introduces and welcomes you before you speak. These episodes often swing between two extremes. Sometimes 'special' speakers (a strange designation in itself) are introduced before they preach as someone who is indeed *special*: while not actually a member of the trinity, the implication is that this speaker certainly is *very* close to the Godhead; they probably have a red telephone on their desk, a hotline to the Master. Their prayers by inference work more efficiently than those of the rest of us plebs, and they have surely committed the book of Numbers to memory. Those who can remember the appalling *Six Million Dollar Man* television character will recall that this bionic chap, blessed as he was with various stainless steel bits, was capable of doing almost anything, as long as he stayed well clear of magnets. While enduring an excessively effusive welcome, I have occasionally wished that I had a few metal appendages myself, seeing as Jeff is 'coming to the pulpit to deliver to us the prophetic *now word* of the Lord, fresh toasty bread straight from heaven's delicious bakery'; whereupon I stand up clutching what feels like the sermonic equivalent of a stale cheese and tomato roll. Of course the other extreme is the cursory, dismissive introduction that suggests that we really don't particularly like the speaker concerned, aren't that bothered that they showed up, and now that they have, may they be hidden behind the cross so that we won't notice them anyway. Occasions like this make me want to peek out from behind the aforementioned cross and wave.

> GOD IS DYNAMICALLY INTERESTED IN WHAT CAN BE SUCH A MUNDANE WORLD

Last week I was introduced by a very nice chap who had previously heard me speak at Spring Harvest: he recounted with delight that I had been dive-bombed while on my way to preach in the big top by a seagull. This low flying bird, which had apparently been out for a few beers and a curry with his seagull mates the night before, pooed right on my head. It was a direct hit and an act of skilful precision.

I had been forced to dash into the nearest loo and wash and blow dry my hair. 'Isn't that great?' the man introducing me chortled, 'That's exactly what I would have done...' Suddenly a super-sharp wit in the congregation shouted out, 'But you can't fly...' It was a brilliant moment, not only because of the quick-on-the-draw response, but also, as everyone giggled and smiled, we remembered that we all live in the very real world, where, whatever the state of my spirituality, seagulls still apparently watch *Dambusters*, faith is sometimes rocked, and headaches and cancers and redundancies and overdrafts still threaten.

The man who introduced me was clearly delighted that the seagull featured in my preaching – and was perhaps a little surprised. Such an event was surely, just so...ordinary; earthy, even?

But life spent as a follower of Jesus allows none of us to graduate from being fundamentally ordinary; neither does it allow us to escape the mundane. He has washed my sins away, but I do still have to clean the car. The good news is that God is dynamically interested and involved in what can be such a mundane world: he refuses to be contained.

Have we created church where we clamour for a rarefied atmosphere, where soaring chords help us 'feel the Spirit?' Do we pop off for a while to never-never land, and then wonder why our faith sometimes seems disconnected from the real world? It's not surprising really, since everyday life doesn't come with backing music. Shutting our eyes to blot out the distractions of this world, do we then confine God to the tiny space between our eyeballs and our eyelids, and forget in the process that God lives and dwells and dances through this world that we seem so keen to blank out?

Georges Bernanos' classic French novel, *The Diary of a Country Priest*[1], ends with the painful death from

[1] Georges Bernanos, translated by P Morris, *The Diary of a Country Priest*, (Fount: 1977)

stomach cancer of the decent young curate – the country priest of the title. Through his difficult life, as recounted in his journal, he appears as a beacon in a dark and dangerous world. The church to which he felt called is beset by corruption and deceit. Bernanos, a devoted Christian and fiercely patriotic Frenchman, presents the good and honest priest as a foil to the excesses of the church of his day. The other priests are self absorbed and seriously flawed, and Christ's reputation suffers at their hands. As the priest lies dying, we are forced to wonder at the harshness of his struggle. He can no longer keep his diary. Another priest has been called to perform the last rites, but has not yet arrived. We discover the fate and the wisdom of the curate through a letter written by the friend who was with him at the very end:

TOUCHES OF GRACE ARE ALL AROUND US

> The priest was still on his way, and finally I was bound to voice my regret that such delay threatened to deprive my comrade of the final consolations of our church. He did not seem to hear me. But a few moments later, he put his hand over mine and his eyes entreated me to draw closer to him. He then uttered these words almost in my ear. And I am quite sure I have recorded them accurately, for his voice, though halting, was strangely distinct. 'Does it matter? Grace is everywhere…' I think he died just then…

The dying priest was right: signs and symbols and touches of grace are all around us, because God wants to *interact* with us. Encounter is at the heart of Christianity as well as faith. Sometimes the word 'experience' is used with suspicion in Christian circles, as if it is legitimate to read *about* God in Scripture and yet not to profoundly encounter him today in any way other than through the pages of the Bible; God locked and bound in his word. But God's revelation is on display everywhere, and he longs to touch us in a myriad of different ways. Certainly we are in need of these touches. In 1917, the German theologian Rudolph Otto wrote that 'modern man cannot even shudder properly.' We seem to have lost the capacity for awe, and instead have turned to look for wonder and thrill in technology – which doesn't satisfy our hunger. On the contrary, as Annie Dillard notes, we are damaged by the endless 'artificial touches' of our modern day living: 'The artificial touches of caffeine, television, fluorescent lights, adrenaline addiction, computers, telephones, bump and scurry and make us restless, excitable, and voracious…'[2]

We need to know, to sense, to encounter and to walk with God. This is not to suggest that Christianity is a journey of daily *explosive* interactions with the divine: often grace is only to be seen by eyes that deliberately focus on God, or heard by ears that seek to hear its faintest whisper. Yet sometimes we ignore him, even when he apparently shouts. In a famous cartoon strip, a character is shown kneeling to pray, saying to God, 'It's not easy to believe in you, God. We never see you. How come you never show yourself? How do we know you even exist?'

At this point a flower springs to life next to him and a volcano erupts in the distance. An eclipse of the sun turns

[2] Chris Blake, *Searching for a God to love*, (W Publishing, 2000)

the sky black and a star shoots across the stratosphere. A tidal wave crashes over him, lightning cracks, a bush begins to burn, a stone rolls away from the entrance of a tomb. He pulls himself from the mud; 'Okay, okay...' he mumbles. 'I give up. Every time I bring up this subject, all we get is interruptions.'

God is near, and he wants to get up close and personal. That truth affects our understanding of the world around us. We have evolved an idea that there are 'laws' of nature – which seem to imply that there is a cold-hearted mechanic or scientist at the heart of the Universe. Nature becomes, not an ongoing act of creation and sustenance, but a machine of necessity. But God continues his second by second play with earth, as a passionate artist.

> He is very much here, and not only when he is acknowledged or noticed. That helps us to understand why a piece of gloriously inventive music may be written by someone who doesn't know God; we can admire the masterful use of colour and shade on canvas, the work of an artist whose heart is in the far country, and yet who has been kissed, though they don't know it, by the touch of the Creator. Shall we ascribe the source of their creativity to Satan? We must not, because we are living in a God-bathed world.[3]

The Jesus who was mistaken for a gardener after his resurrection often shows up in the grey, ordinary things of life. Grace *can* be revealed by great displays of supernatural power; but we are wrong to limit God to the realm of the extraordinary and the remarkable; indeed, those who are

---

[3] Jeff Lucas, *How not to Pray*, (Carlisle; Authentic Lifestyle and Spring Harvest publishing division, 2002)

always on the lookout for signs and miracles can tend to grab hold of the faintest hint of a miracle with an unseemly haste – and God's Name is discredited if the 'miracle' is not authentic. Of course God *has* chosen to do these things throughout history, and continues to do so – but grace is to be found all around us in the ordinary. Thus God can be found in a painting, in a sunrise, in the innocence of a new-born's eyes, in a rosebud or a character in a film or a book, in a song or change of seasons, in the love of our friends, in good food and conversation. We can bump into grace at the coffee shop as well as the church building. 'Faith rules through ordinary things: through cooking and small talk, through storytelling, through making love...all the places where the gravy soaks in, grace shines through.'[4]

GOD CAN BE AT
WORK IN THE
MOST UNEXPECTED
PLACES

But if this is to happen, we must once again attack the myth of the sacred and secular divide, which still prevails in much of our thinking. The tendency is to divide our lives into religious and non-religious categories – things which are *sacred and religious*, (like church attendance, prayer, spiritual reflection, and reading Christian books) and some of which are *secular and therefore spiritually neutral*, like attending football games, sunbathing, driving to work, and watching films.

But the life and methodology of Jesus shows us that grace cannot be so ghettoised; God can be at work in the most unexpected places. An understanding of this will prevent us from developing the view that God is only at

[4] Quoted in Michael Frost, *Seeing God in the Ordinary: a Theology of the Everyday*, (Hendrickson: 2000)

work in the 'Christian' sub culture, and that we must somehow flee from the 'godless' culture that surrounds us. Thus God can reveal himself through our life experiences, through our works of service, through relationships as we become sacraments; through art and creation and coincidence, as well as through the family table of the Eucharist. God wants us to be on the lookout for him on Mondays as well as Sundays.

Grace, creation, and creativity

In the Steven Spielberg film, *The Colour Purple*, Whoopi Goldberg plays a poor, illiterate slave girl. In one scene, she is strolling down a dusty lane with a friend. Beside them runs a gnarled fence, and, beyond that, lies a magnificent purple hill. The purple hill is crowned with a deep blue sky, dotted with clouds at the horizon. Goldberg's character softly nudges her friend and smiles gently, saying, 'See that? That's God making a pass at us.' Am I one who often ignores such an imaginative suitor?

Calvin Seerfield used the phrase 'the hallelujahing of creation' to call us to the recognition that God's creation is a means of revelation and grace. The Bible is emphatic in its assertion that creation is prophetic: it is not itself an object of worship, but it declares the glory of the Creator-designer-sustainer God whose genius it so wonderfully conveys. Our failure to recognise this is nothing short of tragic; it means, to borrow Annie Dillard's phrase, that, 'creation is playing to an empty house.' Creation is ordered to demand a response from us; we do not sigh with wonder at the crashing waves or the snow capped mountains just because we have learned to think that they are attractive. Grace means that creation carries a signature from the Artist, who uses the canvas of land and seascapes, of sunsets and patterns in frost, of colour and texture and smell, to help us reconnect with awe. Perhaps we would know more of grace if we chose more walks in the woods, more time to splash around in the water with our children, more time just to notice things.

> We are here to abet creation and to witness it, to notice each thing so each thing gets noticed. Together, we notice not only the mountain shadow and each stone on the beach, but we notice each other's beautiful face and complex nature so that creation need not play to an empty house.[5]

My good friend and colleague Dary Northrop tells of a time when he was driving in the Colorado Mountains late at night. Realising that he was almost out of petrol, he checked his trip computer, only to be told that he didn't have enough fuel to get him to the next petrol station. He spent the next thirty minutes in a state of complete agitation, worried that he would break down miles from help. Gripping the steering wheel tight, praying hard and sweating harder, he nursed the car on, even slipping it into neutral when going downhill in order to eke out the last few drops of precious fuel. It was a nerve-racking time, but finally, his car coughing in protest, he pulled up at a petrol station, jumped out, and filled the tank to the brim.

---

[5] Annie Dillard, The Meaning of Life, *Life* magazine

'As I stood there, so very relieved, for some reason I decided to look up at the sky – and there was an absolutely beautiful full moon. In all my fretting and agitation, and my gazing at the fuel gauge, I hadn't noticed it...'

Creativity in worship and communication can also 'help us notice.' Some have complained that Christians are too focused on expressing the truth in words, leaving those who prefer other forms and expressions of communication feeling disenfranchised and unable to express their worship and message in any way other than with yet more words, this time set to music. In the last couple of decades, however, there has been a rediscovery of dance, painting, sculpture, poetry, rap and theatre arts in the church. We must welcome this, not as a phase or alternative worship style that appeals to a right-brained few, (and not just because of a few verses in the Old Testament that affirm that the artisans were anointed!) but because God has always designed us to imbibe faith through the senses and not just through the intellect. In terms of revelation, God shows himself afresh through art.

> GOD HAS ALWAYS DESIGNED US TO IMBIBE FAITH THROUGH THE SENSES

> Painting might be a window through which a confused world looks and sees the sane order of God's creation. Music could become an orchestrated echo of the Voice the tired ears of humanity have longed for ages to hear. This is art through which God is seen and heard, in which he is incarnate, is 'fleshed out' in paint and ink, in stone, in creative movement.[6]

---

[6] Michael Card, *Scribbling in the Sand*, (Leicester; IVP, 2002)

Walter Brueggemann, longing for the day when more
creative people will feel increasingly welcome in the
church, quotes poet Walt Whitman who sees Jesus more
as a poet of grace than a salvation technician:

> After all the seas are crossed (as they seem already crossed)
> After the great captains and engineers have accomplished
> their work
> After the noble inventors, after the scientists, the chemist,
> the geologist, ethnologist,
> Finally shall come the poet worthy of that name,
> The true son of God will come singing his songs.[7]

Coincidence and serendipity

What about those times – there are surely many of them
– when we 'just happened' to be in the right place at the
right time? Grace is to be discovered and noticed in the
thankful realisation that God is able to order our steps
for his purpose, which is truly a wonderful idea to con-
template: God, in us, working through us, as we offer
ourselves, not as puppets, but as junior partners to his
purposes.

Despite the dangers that we Christians can find ourselves in if we insist on 'sacramentalising' every event
in our lives and trying to read meaning and message in
each one (a practice that will not only lead to confusion
but possibly poor mental health) – there is no doubt that
God is able to direct circumstances and happenings in

---

[7] Walt Whitman, *Leaves of Grass*, from Walter Brueggemann,
Finally comes the Poet – Daring speech for Proclamation
(Augsburg Fortress publishers, 1990)

our lives so that they become a means of grace to us or others, in terms of a message, or direct us to a situation where we may be of service. Jesus, who walked in the purposes of his Father, 'had to go' through Samaria, and encountered the woman at the well there. Some call these events 'serendipity.' Obviously the ultimate breakthrough of God into our time/space world is the Calvary event; but he continues to interact and engage with us in serendipitous moments, which may not necessary be dramatic or miraculous. These could be:

- The 'chance' meeting with someone that turned out to be a 'divine appointment'

- The sermon or reading from Scripture that just seemed to speak directly into our situation right now

- The 'timely' word of encouragement that brings refreshing and strength to us

- The sense that we have been given wisdom for 'turning point' days that are pivotal in our lives...the Jews have a saying about those life changing days: 'if not for that day...'

We are about to look at the Sabbath, rhythm and rest and its part in being a means of grace to us. But we could somehow rush to the view that it is only in inactive contemplation that God is found. God can also be experienced in the toil and pressure of serving him. Serving provides us with the opportunity to break selfishness, and self absorption.

Pope Gregory I (AD 540-604) dreamed of living a quiet life of contemplation as a monk, but felt in prayer the unyielding call to serve the church – much to his disappointment. He regarded himself as a 'contemplative condemned to action.' But he was dynamically effective following his appointment in 590, selling much of the church's resources to care for the poor who were being decimated by famine and war. He provoked the church to mission, renewed the church's worship life and called the clergy back to a role of being genuine caring 'shepherds of souls.'

> SERVICE IS NOT THE ENEMY OF GRACE AND ITS REVELATION

Service is not the enemy of grace and its revelation. It may well be the source of such revelation, itself a sacrament, as long as our service is balanced and in rhythm. Perhaps we would notice grace more if we consciously offered our hours and days to God, and specifically asked him to direct and use our time here.

Waiting for God

I don't cope well with waiting. For me, the queue is a boring, barren place to be avoided at all costs, and, although I consider myself to be a balanced, compassionate sort, I am inclined towards executing those who jump queues – after making them wait endlessly in line, of course. I desperately try to negotiate waiting in check-in lines at airports with grace, but I often catch myself impatiently tapping my feet like Ringo Starr on Duracells.

Being a full blown quickaholic, I struggled with an internal eruption of silent but smouldering rage when someone pushed in front of me in a pub the other day; they were undeniably rude, but the moral indignation that I felt should really be reserved for headlines about genocide. And being in a rush has other bizarre side effects. I noticed recently that I do not usually dry off completely after showering in the morning; I am powered by an urgent desperation to get on to the next more interesting thing. Thus I usually march into most days breathless as well as slightly damp, having washed my hair with the stuff that contains both shampoo *and* conditioner.

Tonight, I saw a beautiful and profoundly challenging sight. It was more than a glimpse; I studied the lustrous scene for a good while, drinking in its glory. Tonight, I watched as dozens and dozens of young people did something wonderful for God. They waited for him.

The scene was *Summer Madness*, a hugely popular youth event based in Northern Ireland. Thousands of bright young things show up annually, pitch their tents, eat too many hot dogs and probably take too few showers, and generally have an all round good time which includes going bonkers about Jesus. There's a heady cocktail of arts, fun, teaching, and worship all served up with the winsome Irish ability to enjoy a bit of *craic*. And this is more than a Bible bless-up; the main event is followed by something called StreetReach; four days of showing cast-iron kindness in one of the hardest areas of the Shankhill. *Madness* is about clean hearts and very dirty hands. Last night I was privileged to be the speaker there.

At the end of the service, these young people came forward for prayer in droves, their response quick and uninhibited. Members of the prayer team moved smilingly and swiftly through the throng, sharing a few holy moments in prayer and, in some cases, in tears. But a tender moment of care takes time – the prayer team was outnumbered: people would have to wait.

꽃 꽃

And wait they did. Their waiting was costly, for this was the first night of the event; time to get back to the tent and cremate some beans on toast over the Bunsen; time to get with their mates, to head for a late

I AM ACTUALLY
IMPATIENT TO BE
PATIENT... ZAP ME,
GOD...

꽃 꽃

night concert or chat show ... but they laid all of that aside, and waited. And I watched, and wondered.

I pondered the thought that most of us live in a Nescafe culture of 'give it to me now', and have now developed a mutated vision of a McGod whom we expect to serve up rapid fire blessing in a drive through church, right now, as you like it, have a nice day says the Lord. Has the word *faith* become confused with the word *now*?

Even as I write this, I am struck by the irony that I am actually impatient to be patient. Zap me, God, nuke me, turbo-charge me, but please don't make me wait in line in that painful slow crucible where character is forged.

Fear not, nervous reader, for I am not advocating that you move to a semi-detached hermit's cave and there prance around in sackcloth; my call is more simply that we give God a bit of that which is viewed as one of our most precious possessions – the gift of some time.

Meanwhile, back in the fast lane, today I saw a newspaper ad announcing the arrival of a no-wait video recorder, where we can watch the beginning of a film before the machine has even finished recording the end. Hooray, hallelujah, and eureka. How did we ever live without it?

ꙅ ꙅ

SPIRITUALITY
INVOLVES
STILLNESS

ꙅ ꙅ

We are a people on the run. A New York City subway token booth attendant spends most of her day watching the passengers. 'They like to run', she says. 'They don't feel right if they don't run. This is what I watch; the rat race. I watch them run to work, and I watch them run home…' None of us need to be reminded that we are living faster than ever – we are 'quickaholics' – which carries a high toll. We live in a daily avalanche of sensory overload in what Bob Dylan describes as the 'fury of the moment.'

The apocalyptic visions of literary prophets have come to pass, although not entirely as we – or they – anticipated. In 1985, Neil Postman published *Amusing Ourselves to Death* to denounce the decline of the Age of Typography and the ascent of the Age of Television. The book's Foreword contrasts two negative utopias, the dark vistas of George Orwell's *1984* and Aldous Huxley's *Brave New World*. While many view the books as parallel creations by British contemporaries, notable differences arise. Orwell spoke of a future when books would be banned; Huxley saw a horizon where there would be no reason to ban a book, no need to conceal truth – because it would be drowned by irrelevance and information overload, the result of a trivial culture.

As we check our bulging email boxes, and download yet more useless information from the internet, it's now evident who was more correct. Running means that we fail to think properly. Postman laments that today's TV news 'creates the illusion of knowing something but in fact leads one away from knowing.' He goes on to lament the death of meaningful discourse: 'In court-rooms, classrooms, operating rooms, board rooms, churches and even aeroplanes, people no longer talk to each other, they entertain each other. They do not exchange ideas; they exchange images. The shocking future is present.'

Such rush means that we often fail to see the tokens of grace and God that are everywhere. We need to learn to open our eyes wide open, an idea popularised by Robert Fulghum's book *All I really needed to know I learned in kindergarten*, a best-seller that resonated with millions around the world.

'Remember the Dick and Jane books and the first word you learned, the biggest word of all…LOOK![8]

Spirituality – which is about *looking* – involves still-ness: Abraham Heschel says that 'To pray is to stand still and know how to dwell upon a word.' If we fail to learn how to stop for a while, we will miss so much grace.

Sabbath and rhythm

If we are to navigate our way through this world empowered by and envisioned by grace, then this will

---

[8] Robert Fulghum, *All I really needed to know I learned in kindergarten*, (Ballantine Books, 2003)

only happen as we take deliberate steps to build rhythm, pause, rest and reflection into each of our days. The shorthand word for this is Sabbath. It is not my purpose here to discuss our theologically distinctive approaches to Sabbath; sadly the word has become associated with the obsessive, legalistic practices of the Puritans and earlier Constantinian legislation rather than the provision of God for a rounded life. How we achieve that will involve variety and creativity. Suffice it to say that the Sabbath principle was given to provide:

- Rest and inactivity

- Shift from the sameness of work into other activities

- Celebration – a popular saying among early Christians was 'Sunday we give to joy'

- Getting renewed perspective on ourselves – the Sabbath is a recognition that we are not indispensable, (the world will continue to turn as we rest!) and is an antidote to legalistic striving

- Friendship, fellowship and familial togetherness

- Replenishment and refreshment, not only for humans, but for animals and land – an environmental Sabbath

- Prayer and reflection

God is restful. If we are to experience grace everywhere, we will need to make decisions to slow down, make friends again with silence, and find creative ways to embrace the Sabbath principle of pause.

John Ortberg, author of *The Life you always wanted*, calls for a relentless commitment to 'slowing' – eliminating hurry and 'hurry sickness' from our lives with a series of determined choices. Ortberg affirms that 'hurry is a disordered heart.'

We need to stop long enough to think about how we are doing life, as it were. Are we frantic by nature, constantly speeding up our daily activities – and looking with tension for the smallest line in the supermarket, or a sense of impatience at the red traffic light that delays us for 45 seconds?

Do we multi-task without notice that we are doing it – driving a car, drinking coffee, talking (hands free!) on the telephone, monitoring the radio, applying make-up and making 'friendly' gestures to fellow motorists – all at the same time? Are our lives characterised by clutter, as we gather books and magazines, which we don't have time to read – and   accumulating time saving devices which we don't have time to learn how to operate? Are our email boxes bulging, our appointments missed and our projects usually unfinished?

Is it our view that we just don't have time for friendships?

Do our days end with begin and end with a feeling of exhaustion – sunrise and sunset fatigue, dominated by television – where we are unable to converse or communicate and we turn tasks that should be a pleasure into races against the clock? ('okay, children, let's see who can take their bath fastest!')

Let's learn to slow down, chew our food before swallowing it, and deliberately drive in the slow lane (or better, take the country route), dump our watches for a while, and choose the long queue at the supermarket. Let's turn off that mobile phone for a week, and realise that there is seductiveness about being needed – it makes us feel important. Slowing brings us back to face that insecurity that we might well be dispensable.

Let's smell the coffee, linger for prayer, check out the moon, remember to laugh and notice the birds. And, based on my experience with a low flying seagull, if you spot one of our feathered friends with a bomb sight attached to its backside, take cover immediately.

6

I WILL COMMIT MYSELF TO THE JOYS AND PAINS OF CHURCH

Gauguin says that when sailors have to move
a heavy load or raise an anchor, they all sing
together to keep them up and give them vim.
That is just what artists lack.
Vincent Van Gogh

Give me a 'J'

I t was one of those fireside, late in the evening, 'tell
us your most embarrassing moment' chats over a
glass of vintage juice and a wedge of decomposing
Stilton. The anecdote that my friend Alistair told had us
all in agony; as he relived his worst moment, we vicari-
ously cringed with him.

It happened when he was a bright Christian young
thing attending a Cliff Richard concert at the Royal
Albert Hall in London. Sitting in that huge cavernous
building, and waiting for a younger Cliff to come on
stage to perform, my enthusiastic pal was suddenly
kissed by utter madness. The idea dawned in his zealous
head that he would just stand up and lead the crowd in
one of those 'Jesus shouts' … you know the routine:
'give me a J, give me an E', etc.

These moments of spontaneous cheerleading are
always dangerous, particularly if the name that one is

asking everyone to 'give you' is quite long. The word 'Jesus', being but five letters, is normally a safe bet for this little bit of responsive activity; plus, a crowd of Christians would feel obliged, required even, to holler back a throaty and jolly retort, on the basis of the shout being for, well, Jesus...

⮜ ⮞

CHURCH... IS BOTH
IMPERFECT AND
GLORIOUS

⮜ ⮞

Longer names are more challenging. One should never ask even the kindliest crowd to give you an 'M' for Melchizedek, or Malahalashasbaz. Enthusiasm is likely to fade faster than the Pope playing squash. But a shout for Jesus from Christians is normally going to be forthcoming, especially when nothing else interesting is afoot. And so, emboldened by the still Cliff-less stage, Alistair stood to his feet, punched the air with gusto and with a high pitched yell, invited twenty thousand people to give him a 'J'. The expected deafening roar failed to materialise; around 450 of the keener types dutifully provided the requested 'J'. Feeling a little disappointed, yet hopeful for a better second letter, my erstwhile enthusiastic pal invited everyone to give him an 'E', whereupon around ninety would-be martyrs, all of whom were probably wearing sandals *and* socks at the time, provided the hapless crowd conductor with a half-hearted 'E'. By the time it got to the first 'S', only a faithful group of around twelve faithful disciples could bring themselves to offer a now dispirited response that was more a corporate mumble than a yell, and their subdued offering was probably drowned out by the sound of thousands of sets of buttocks slamming together in acute embarrassment. There would never be a 'U'. It was time, surely, for Alistair to sit down, and acknowledge defeat, which he did, his face flushed a fluorescent crimson. And as he sat, his friends edged away a little, wanting to put some distance between them and the now retired and indeed ineffective group captain. Confusion settled upon people who were up in the 'gods' of the hall, who wanted to know why they were all being asked to give a shout for Jess.

Tears of mirth ran down our faces as we remembered the folly of younger, more zealous days. We cringed at our brash, clumsy evangelistic sorties; and we laughed out loud at some of the ridiculous and theologically bankrupt songs that we must have enjoyed, way back then. We marvelled at the former superficiality that enabled us to sing certain lyrics, like one spiritual ditty that dealt with the problem of pain in a manner probably unrivalled by C. S. Lewis:

> We want everybody to be happy
> We want everybody to be glad
> We want everybody to be happy in the Lord
> And we don't want anybody sad.

We in turns marvelled and mocked our yesteryears. But there was something blended into our conversation that enabled us to avoid cynicism or unkindness – and that was our shared gratitude for this wonderful, irritating, thrilling, embarrassing, and precious thing called church; for she is both imperfect and glorious. One after another we shared stories about victories and defeats, breakthroughs and struggles. We laughed about the Easter Play held by one large church where one of the crucified thieves yelled at Jesus, 'If you're the Son of God, save yourself and us!' and then promptly fell off his cross. We realised, too, that the church in her failure is not separate from us: her embarrassments are *our* embarrassments, as we own some responsibility for the collective strengths and weaknesses to which we all, as individuals, contribute. But as the fire burned down to fading embers, we toasted one of the most wonderful and most demanding inventions that God has come up with to date; church.

Called to be together

Grace calls us together – both as part of the community called church, and as part of the wider community of humanity. God's grace brings us to tough choices about the rugged demands of relationship, as we are invited to live as gracious servants in a world that can be characterised by conflict and grabbing. Solitary faith might occasionally be tempting, but simply won't work. The decision to become a follower and an apprentice of Jesus is a personal choice; but language such as 'Jesus is now my personal Saviour' can lead to an aberrational view of salvation; that it is an individualised experience and that the church exists only to nurture that one-on-one relationship that we now enjoy with God through Christ. But God deals with a salvation people, not persons. Just as he was the one who saved and delivered the Hebrews soon to become Israel, so he calls us to live out grace lives together as part of the community that is the church. As they were led forward out of Egypt into a promised land of rest, so the church is the *ekklesia*, the mobile community who have done far more than 'asked Jesus into their hearts' – we have signed up for a journey under the leadership of the Christ who calls us to follow him together. And a costly journey it is. Just as Moses occasionally felt despair at all the pettiness and wrangling of those early trekkers, so there are times when a walk alone looks good to us as well.

C S Lewis wrote of the sacrificial decision he made to choose fellowship over isolation. Initially he had believed that he could be a solitary Christian: that he didn't need to go to church or to sing hymns, which he disliked. But by going to church, by meeting people who were very different to himself, he began to realise that he did need others and that he wasn't, perhaps, quite as saintly as he had thought.

GRACE CALLS US
TOGETHER

For some reason we still live with a sense of surprise when we are disappointed by church; surely, without giving way to being jaundiced, cynical people, we need to be a little more realistic about the fact that church is comprised of people very much like us – incomplete folk under construction, those still very much in the process. The church has given us great gifts like Albert Schweitzer, Eric Liddell, Martin Luther King and Mother Teresa. She has also given us the Crusades and Jim Jones, who began his ministry as an effective and respected Christian leader. We need grace, and we need to offer grace. The church is not a trophy case, but a field hospital. During the Protestant Reformation there was much debate as to whether the church was a *school for saints* or a *hospital for sinners*. But the church, while called to be a beacon of prophetic hope, is not a community of the perfectly accomplished, but rather a gathering of those being perfected and honed. Luther and

Calvin actually rejected the 'school for saints' model and adopted the 'hospital' imagery instead. While we reach out for growth and maturity, we recognise that we are the 'now and not yet' eschatological community, and should not be surprised to discover other sinners – like us – who are still very much on the pathway of finding kingdom life, health and growth in their lives.

Yet there is huge potential in this gathering of the incomplete, as we 'gaze upon God' together. God has surely designed things so that we should be able to discern and celebrate the acts of God in each other's lives as we travel together in fellowship C S Lewis demonstrated in his writings that the church is a community of people, each of whom is gifted to see God differently, in an unique way that they can then bless others with. We see God, not only in our acts of worship but by fully opening our eyes in friendship and fellowship.

Perhaps we need to rediscover what used to be called 'the testimony time', which largely fell into disuse because dear old Doris was always thanking the Lord for healing her chilblains, (which seemed to come back on Monday morning, must have been the devil) or because young Pete tended to drop a swearword into his testimony every time he took the microphone. But in a world apparently obsessed with reality television and in order that we can truly discover God's beauty in each other, the church must be courageous and break the notion that truth is only to be handled by the ordained and trained professionals – and release the power of community hermeneutics – the telling of our own stories. The widow will be far more able to share her experience of grace in the face of loneliness and grief than the trained preacher who skims through the concordance looking for the word 'lonely'. Without this we face the weekly absurdity of 'expert' advice from people who know little or nothing of the reality of the pain about which they speak – a particularly frustrating prospect for those who are negotiating pain. The American theologian Stanley Hauerwas, in his book *A community of character*[1], affirms the need for the church to rediscover itself as a story formed community. Nelson Mandela's autobiography, *Long March to Freedom*[2], tells of how he was impacted by people's stories as a boy, which then sustained him through his long years of imprisonment. Auschwitz survivor Elie Weisel was similarly upheld through his mistreatment at the hands of the Nazis by recalling the Hassidic stories of his tradition.

THE CHURCH IS
NOT A TROPHY
CASE BUT A FIELD
HOSPITAL

In the last few days I have bumped into an impressive number of heroes – none of whom looked noteworthy if one just glanced at them, for they were not draped in designer clothing, nor surrounded by paparazzi with popping flashbulbs. Last weekend I met, for the first time, a couple whose son has just been charged with murder. He has been on remand, and now, this week, they have been asked to open their home to him once again as a condition of bail. Meeting them was an encounter with two heroes who are currently navigating their way through what is surely every parent's nightmare: I tried to imagine what it

---

[1] Stanley Hauerwas, *A Community of Character: Towards a constructive Christian social ethic*, (University of Notre Dame Presse, 1981)
[2] Nelson Mandela, *Long Walk to Freedom*, (Abacus, 1995)

would feel like, if I ended *my* day by switching out the light on my bedside cabinet, knowing that *my* son was holed up in the musty echoing of a overcrowded cell, the slamming of doors by the dozen and the shouts and yells of derision his goodnight lullaby.

Then there is the young Anglican vicar who has been diagnosed with an aggressive cancer. As a marathon runner, he has decided to run the race with Jesus all the way, whatever the outcome. His is not the faith of the grinning television evangelist who promises ease, health and wealth with the signing of a cheque made payable to himself. Rather this is a long distance faith that looks into the eyes of the wife who stands bravely, hopefully at his side, as he paces around yet another hospital waiting room, summoned to hear the results of yet another batch of tests, scribbles on a report that will tell him that he will live to see his children grown, or that he will die soon. He reaches out in the darkness, for the light that is God; and as he reaches, he is a hero.

ARE WE BUILDING A CHURCH WHERE DISCOVERY... DISAGREEMENT AND DIALOGUE ARE WELCOME?

Then I bumped into a lady with lined but smiling eyes, who has a son who is homosexual and has tested HIV positive. Now she seeks to reach out to other mothers in this harrowing position to offer care and support. She does so knowing that her son is opposed to her Christian beliefs, and so has to be somewhat secretive about her attempts to bring comfort to others, but she quietly determines to push through the pain barrier anyway. Extraordinary.

All around us there are these truly incredible people, who are not superhuman, nor known by many, yet are filled with courage, kindness and grace. As I meet them and listen to their stories, my vision of the God who sustains them is enlarged.

Church as a space for grace

If the idea of a 'gazing at grace church' is to be more than just a romantic notion, then we are faced with some serious challenges about how we 'do' church. For example, are we building church where discovery, question, disagreement and dialogue are welcomed as tools for true growth – or do we just gather to swallow microwaved, easy answers, like a fast food joint serving up pre-packaged 'truth'?

Walter Brueggeman used the idea of the church as a 'space for grace' in the 1989 Lyman Beecher Lecture at Yale University, and called the church to be a people who 'create poetry in a prose flattened world'. Brueggeman was insisting that the church must use language to surprise, to inquire, to relieve, rather than to batter and compete. He called for danger, newness and dialogue to characterise the church. We use the phrase 'seeker sensitive' to describe a certain approach to church; yet this suggests that the 'saved' have somehow graduated from seeking, and have instead become those who have found the truth in its entirely and have got God all figured out – hence the nervousness amongst some Christians when U2's Bono sang 'I still haven't found what I'm looking for'. Steve Chalke comments:

In his book, *The Challenge of Jesus*, N T Wright tells the story of a theological student in Kenya who listened intently to a lecture given by a European professor about the search for the historical Jesus. Bemused and frustrated, the student suddenly burst in to the flow of the lecture, 'If the Europeans have lost Jesus, that is their problem. We have not lost him. We know him. We love him. We don't need to search for him.' However, as appealing as this kind of certainty might at first sound, it is in fact rather like the presumed familiarity of which Dallas Willard spoke. To assume that we have got Jesus 'pinned down' or 'summed up' is not simply arrogant but stupid, and in the end inhibits our ability to communicate his unchanging message to an ever-changing world.

The consistent and continual use of parables in the teaching ministry of Jesus demonstrates that he was not seeking to 'dumb down' everything about the kingdom of God by using simplistic little stories, but rather was seeking to stimulate seekers after grace to journey after truth, to activate them to a search and to provoke their curiosity. The parables weren't the end of a search, but a green light that signalled the beginning of one. The quest that the church has for relevance should not mean that it reduces everything to a series of 'pat' answers to complex questions. It will seek to equip, while remaining at ease with mystery. 'Gazing' at the God of grace will be quite impossible without this quality. Are we a church that is unafraid of difficult questions?

A lot of what takes place in pulpits and Sunday Schools … is really about taking the search out of learning. We're too used to having the answers packaged for us. We're never asked to look. Our curiosity is never pricked, our interest never aroused. We sit through sermons in a daze, half listening, lost in our own thoughts. When was the last time a sermon, a Bible Study, or a Sunday School class got under your skin and activated such an interest that you felt compelled to mediate upon the matter, to *meditate* research or explore an issue, to question others or to search for your own views? When sermons end, we close our Bibles. When was the last time you heard a sermon and went home and opened your Bible to discover more?[3]

Are we willing to be provoked, stirred, and sometimes stunned and confronted by truth as the story of God is danced, sculpted, spoken, painted, mimed, sung and rhymed? Are we a church that demands that its communicators comfort more than confront, viewing the sermon that 'offends' as something evil?

Worship will obviously help our gazing: worship is not a consumer product, or a style/fashion choice, but an opportunity through song/creed/ritual/celebration/silence to consider the drama of salvation and the instigator of it, our God. Worship will help grace communities into a habit of gratitude rather than grumbling, and help us once again gather around the Father of all us: the fact that makes us truly family. Is our church giving itself wholeheartedly to worship, or does it view corporate worship as a mere preliminary to the 'really important' business of the day – namely, the sermon? If the grace found in Jesus Christ is our primary message, then surely the way that we gather in his name will reflect a sense of space and freedom.

[3] Michael Frost, *Seeing God in the Ordinary: A Theology of the Everyday*, (Hendrickson, 2000)

Humanity mingled with spirituality

I touched on this in the last chapter as we consider grace revealed through the ordinary, but it's worth visiting the need for churches where reality and humanity are celebrated – where authenticity is anticipated. I find that I get into trouble quite a lot as a preacher when I simply confess to being human. Indeed, I was quite taken aback when visiting the toilet before speaking in a church; a chap in there noticed that I was making use of the facilities, and blurted out, 'I'm surprised to see you in here...' What arrangements does he think that we Christian leaders make when it comes to the usual bodily functions?

Perhaps we are fearful of what might happen if we are real; or we are bewildered, refusing to see holiness as a journey, and confusing the call for us to be an example with projecting the right image. Is our church a place where we feel able to be us – or does it seem that everyone feels pressured to project the 'right' image? And are we building church where real humans – and thoroughly proficient sinners – are genuinely welcomed, and allowed to journey rather than instantly being fed into an ever churning discipleship machine? The church that I am privileged to be part of in Colorado had two opportunities to extend such a welcome.

Nicky was a stripper, a bright pre-law student who had discovered that men can be stupid enough – her words – to pay large sums of money to watch women undress. Over a period of months, the man who cut her hair and fixed her nails befriended her and never 'made any moves' – something that surprised her and prompted her to ask why. Wasn't he attracted to her? Larry, the hairdresser, gently let her know that he was a Christian and that his motives were honourable: would she like to go to a church meeting with him?

Nicky sat through her first service whispering and muttering behind cupped hands into the patient Larry's ear. Apparently she thought that the speaker had been given advance notice that she was going to attend, seeing as he seemed to be speaking directly to her. How else was he to know what was going on in her life, and be able to speak so clearly into her situation? Larry whispered that it was probably God working overtime: no one had supplied the preacher with advance intelligence. At the end of the meeting she made a public response to Jesus Christ. She read the New Testament twice through that week, and eventually called the pastor, who was somewhat surprised to be getting a call from a stripper. She was about to change career.

> ARE WE WILLING TO BE PROVOKED, STIRRED AND SOME-TIMES STUNNED BY TRUTH?

'I've been reading that Corinthian book', Nicky said over the phone. 'Have you read that one?' The pastor affirmed that he had indeed read Paul's first epistle to his friends at Corinth. 'It says there that our bodies are the temple of the Holy Spirit. That means that Jesus doesn't want me to work as a stripper, does he?' With a cough, the minister agreed: that would be right.

'I've also read that bit where it says that God will provide for all my needs in the Matthew book. So...he will take care of me if I stop stripping, won't he, with my rent and student debts and all...'

The pastor assured Nicky that God would indeed honour her for making obedient choices, and God did: some years later she is still faithfully serving the Lord. Her baptism was interesting, in that around thirty of her friends from the club, including bra-less strippers in micro-skirts and some rather beefy bouncers, walked down the centre aisle and parked themselves on the front row. Twelve of them came to Christ that night. One of the church people was unimpressed, made an appointment to see the pastor, and said, 'You've ruined our church by allowing *these* people here.' I would have been tempted to floor her with a rebuke, but the pastor was wiser than I: 'I know. I don't know what to do. Will you help me to sort this all out?' The lady thought it over, and ended the meeting by saying 'Oh well, I suppose we are just going to have to love them.' And to her credit, she did just that. But notice that both sinners and saints – on different journeys – were allowed space to grow and travel.

Then there was George, a huge, hard man who loved to fight. He had a well earned reputation for foul language and mean behaviour, and so had tattooed his life message on his knuckles: the left fist had a word that began with 'f', and the right hand concluded the message; 'off'. He wore his message to the world, straight from the heart, on his hands. For some reason he decided to come to a church meeting, and sat with his fists under his chin, glowering at everybody. An older lady walked right over to him and said, 'I don't believe I've met you before. May I give you a hug?' Before he could answer, she threw her arms around this big bear of a man. He said nothing, and couldn't because the tears just poured out of him, his muscled shoulders shaking as he wept like a baby.

A new Christian, he still had his unfortunate message on those gnarled knuckles, which usually only created an issue when he raised his hands in worship. But he was unable to find a job – no employer wanted to hire a man with those words scrawled in crude black ink upon his body. Finally George asked for help, and an offering was taken so that he could have laser surgery to eradicate that old message for good. On the day on his baptism, he held his hands high as he stood in the tank and, weeping again, he shouted, over and over, 'I'm clean, I'm clean!' Neither of these true stories could have happened in church that was committed to looking for a better class of sinner.

> WE'RE JUST GOING TO HAVE TO LOVE THEM

But there are also others who can sometime find themselves feeling like aliens among us, and therefore receive a message of ungrace. All cultures and communities tend to set a standard of so-called (and mythical) 'normality' which can exclude and disenfranchise those who do not fit the stereotypical pattern, which is not actually 'normality' at all, but rather just a default type. The grace church will always treat people as people, not objects – or even vision fodder or foot soldiers! Leadership will also be inclusive. Are we, the church, modelling full inclusivity to, for example, people with disabilities (aware as we must be that having a disability is a very 'normal' part of the human condition and one that we all might face at some time), or do we make their lives more laborious with our bad theologies of healing, our inaccessible buildings, and our insistence that power should always be in the hands of the 'able bodied'? Are single people treated to our ill-advised questions about whether or not they 'have found the right one yet', our clumsy match-making attempts, or our quiet suspicions that they might not be heterosexual? We are all sinful, messed-up humans; and we need a grace church that will throw a party for all of us.

We're all celebrities – get us out of here

Such a church will be filled with people who have the hearts of servants, a strange sight indeed in our fame and status hungry world. Becoming a celebrity is the new rainbow's end that many seem to be chasing. It sometimes appears that we have an entire culture lining up, eager to claim their allotted fifteen minutes of fame; a desire that is certainly force-fed to us by television. The obsession with celebrity is nothing new: Americans of an earlier generation watched aghast as perfectly decent people publicly humiliated themselves for reality television 'groundbreaking' programming like *The Gong Show*, or *The Dating Game*, (which served as the 'inspiration' for our very own *Blind Date*). For those privileged souls who have not yet witnessed this debacle over which our Cilla presided, *Blind Date* enables us to marvel at hapless contestants who weekly thrilled with their innuendo ridden quips as they waited behind the screen – although many of those 'spontaneous' comments, we were told, might well be the dubious work of scriptwriters behind the scenes. Whether it's the national obsession with football, the royal family, whether a Brit will ever win Wimbledon, who won the last reality TV show, or the trailer park gladiatorial games which are the *Jerry Springer show*, we are apparently a people eager to be somebody, even if it means savaging our friends/partners before millions in order to get into that fleeting spotlight. The creator of the now curiously antiquated *Gong Show* remarked that contestants were willing to betray each other for the prize of a few seconds of fame – or infamy – and a free refrigerator: thirty pieces of silver reinvented.

∾ ∾

THE GRACE CHURCH WILL ALWAYS TREAT PEOPLE AS PEOPLE

∾ ∾

Of course, the problem with the celebrity obsession is that it is all quite simply a con. These people may stand in the glare of the lights, but they are basically ordinary folks who are required to deodorise their armpits with the rest of us. Their being so very special owes little to anything other than the well oiled media and publicity machinery that feeds the myth.

But Jesus calls us to another aspiration: to become servants, like him. I have come to believe that the only way to navigate your way through church life – or indeed, any human relationship – is as a servant. Those who receive grace through the suffering servant are called to exemplify that grace by living servant lives. Servanthood does not mean embracing a servile, self-effacing attitude. Rather, as we are willing to be faithful in the mundane, allowing ourselves the freedom to be interrupted, we learn the difficult lesson of being a servant. As we willingly embrace our weaknesses and limitations, 'hold our tongues' when criticised or attacked, refuse to see 'serving' as a subtle means towards recognition, and practically take steps to bear one another's burdens, so the heart of the servant is slowly, painfully formed in us. Ironically, there is liberation in serving, in that the servant recognises that there is a Master who is in control – thus the weight of the world does not rest upon *them*.

THERE IS
LIBERATION IN
SERVING

Servanthood can at times be used to disarm and shame the oppressor – the 'pouring of hot coals' upon someone's head. Walter Wink tells of a black South African woman who was walking on the street with her children when a white man spat in her face. She stopped and said, 'Thank you, and now for the children.' Nonplussed, the man was unable to respond. Of course, there's only one way to find out if you and I are truly servant hearted – and that is to gauge our reaction when people treat us like servants. The revelation that church does not exist for us, but for God and for his kingdom purposes, must dawn on us all if we are to avoid jumping around from one church to another, always searching for something better. We are told to forbear with each other for good reason – there will be things to forbear!

But allow me to add a word of caution here: sometimes people are misused and even abused under the guise that 'we all need to learn to serve'. Just today I received a sobering email from a young lady who is obviously very dedicated to serving her church, but seems to be suffering as a result. I share it with permission, as a salutary reminder that we need to take care that we don't exploit the willing and faithful, and use biblical verses to justify that exploitation.

> Sometimes there seems to be a tendency to abuse – over-use is perhaps a better word – the people who do have faith in their churches. I can't believe that I am the only one that has a problem like this, but then may be I am. I am my church's youth worker and children's worker, I am the child protection officer, I lead the worship on most Sundays either during the whole service or before we go out or come in, and I tend to be the general dogsbody for being roped into other jobs throughout the week or on a Sunday morning.
>
> The problem is, I don't get any spiritual input for myself – it all tends to be output. What I get I do on my own which is okay to a point, but I am actually quite tired most of the time as this is all done on a voluntary basis as I am actually training to be a teacher!
>
> I have tried saying no, but it doesn't work, people come out with comments such as,'Well What Would Jesus Do?' That's not a very Christian thing to do or say!
>
> The worst thing is, (and I do apologize for pouring it all out on to you) that it makes me so angry and upset, that sometimes I hate the thought of going to church! I have started to go to a different church on a Sunday evening where no one knows me and it is lovely, but I shouldn't feel like that about going to my place of worship!

I suggested that, when asked 'What would Jesus do', she respond by answering Jesus was in fact very good at saying 'no' – as well as 'come apart and rest for a while'. She should try the same: if there was no response, perhaps she should look for another church family.

Faithfulness with discernment needed

The grace choice to commit ourselves to the painful rough and tumble of community life is one we should all embrace. But one further word of caution needs to be added, lest these thoughts be used to control or manipulate us into staying in a church that we really need to leave. There are definitely times when we need to say goodbye to a church that has become unhealthy and dominating: faithfulness is not slavish loyalty to that which is wrong.

A friend of mine has seen spiritual abuse first hand. It's subtle. His story demonstrates that you can be in an abusive church and not really be aware of it. The problem is that everyone is afraid to speak out – it takes a lot of self-confidence to go against the rest of the group. He put together a series of tell-tale signs to watch for if you are worried that your church is drifting in this direction. Be assured – the drift is all too easy. Probably no leader decides one day to become controlling. Gradually, imperceptibly, over a period of years the rot sets in.

Ask yourself some questions:

- Is the leadership truly accountable to anyone?

- Do your leaders preach submission to their authority – regardless of whether you think they are wrong or right?

- Does your leader ever admit to being wrong? If so, does he/she apologise to those who have been wronged and seek not to do the same things again?

- Does your leader claim to hear God for everyone in the congregation?

- Does your leader claim your church has been singled out by God for special favour? Is the message really that God is only interested in your church (or group of churches)?

- Are other churches/ministries dismissed as backslidden?
- Are those chosen for leadership all of one mind on authority?

- Do you have difficulty in separating your relationship with God from your relationship with the leader?

- Is there a strong culture of secrecy in the church?

- How does the leadership deal with those who criticise it? Are they marginalised, bullied or viewed as being problem people?

- Does the leader take every opportunity to impress the church with his spiritual credentials – how long he prays for each morning, etc?

- Are those who leave the church told that God will never bless them again?

- When people leave, is the statement made that God is 'pruning the church' or 'getting rid of the chaff'?

- Are those who leave the church ever mentioned again?

Whatever the positive side, if these things are true of your church, be warned. Any leaders who put themselves into this position are in danger of setting themselves up as idols. Few churches will exhibit all of these signs: but just because your church only has a couple, it doesn't mean you shouldn't be concerned. Get outside advice and support – and be prepared for a long haul. Leaving an abusive church can mean leaving many of your friends behind – one of the signs of an abusive church is that those who leave find themselves ostracised by those who remain. Recovery takes time – and should do so: leaving a church is not something we should do lightly.

The tragedy of the controlling church is that it discredits one of the most beautiful experiences that we can ever enjoy: the joy of being part of a church family. To come in from the cold of isolation and aloneness, and sit by that warm hearth of fellowship, is one of the great grace gifts that God has so richly provided for us.

7

I WILL DETERMINE TODAY TO BE
A MEANS OF GRACE TO OTHERS

The world is really sick. I just wanted to see if the
world could really change.
Trevor MacKinney in *Pay it Forward*

He (or she) who does not love is not just a bad
Christian. They are not a Christian at all.
F.F. Bruce

Leaving graffiti behind

We were on Gozo, Malta's little sister island. The sun was a gigantic, blistering fireball framed by a cloudless azure sky, the relentless heat creating that surreal shimmer that makes the whole world ripple very slightly. With much brow wiping and gasping, we trudged on up the hill towards the Gozo Temple, which, we were told, was a must see. These were *probably* the oldest free standing buildings in the world, being over five thousand years old even when Jesus was still in swaddling cloths. I was tempted to abandon the cultural experience in favour of a pint of *probably* the best lager in the world. But we pushed on, dust swirling around our sandals and pebble-dashing our tongues. This Temple had better be good.

And good it was. As a history Philistine who has been known to discourage visiting Americans from going to Stonehenge ('just a pile of well arranged elderly rocks') and the Tower of London ('seen one tin can suit of armour, seen 'em all'), I am not usually too enthralled with ancient sights, but this one certainly fired my imagination, which went into overdrive as we meandered around those Methuselah stones. I wondered what unspeakable things had been done in these flinty cloisters, what innocent blood had dribbled down over still erected altars, what bizarre rituals had been perpetuated here in the name of now forgotten gods. I peered across the roped barrier at the intricate arrangement of rocks that had been placed there seven millennia earlier, and then marvelled at an unmistakable inscription hewn deep into one of the larger stones: 'West Ham United'. A chiselling from a more recent visitor, I assumed, dismissing the possibility that our prehistoric forefathers had prophetically raised a cheer for the lads from Upton Park. There were other, classier graffiti offerings, including one from Robert, who back in 1848 had left his name in neat gothic script.

OUR LIVES
CREATE GRAFFITI
EVERY SECOND

Why do we all seem to harbour such a desire to let complete strangers know that we have been this way, this hankering to mark our passing by? Graffiti is a strange manifestation; perhaps the oddest of all is the evangelical scribbling much in evidence on British motorway bridges. Everyone driving north up the M1 now has the opportunity to know that *Jesus is Lord*, courtesy of some grinning enthusiast who was blessed with a pot of white paint and sadly not over-blessed with a sizeable brain. (I'll brace myself for the letter from an irate reader who will no doubt write to share with us the good news that he did indeed cry out 'What must I do to be saved?' as a result of espying this gospel graffiti whilst speeding up to Scotland).

But our lives create graffiti every second, our signature is everywhere: in the way we work, in our treatment of friends and enemies, in the manner in which we do church. No wonder the New Testament warns those of us who are leaders to scribble carefully, as those whose jottings will attract more 20/20 scrutiny and judgement on the final day; for we have an awesome opportunity to beautify – or deface – the lives of those who trust us. And something more precise than doodling is required of parents, for children are wet cement. It's an extreme example, but I recently spent a harrowing evening with a fine young couple who had found a better future in Jesus after the wife had endured years of systematic rape and abuse at the hands of her 'Christian leader' dad. That pious, scripture quoting freak vandalised the very term 'father', and gouged his name deep into the heart, mind – and body – of his precious daughter, who should have been safe in the arms of her daddy. He continues to deflower her daily with his adamant protests of innocence: his is an autograph signed in lurid, indelible ink.

But the positive is also true: that all of us are gifted with the mysterious blessing called influence: the chance to strengthen and bless: to scribble our initials as we go out of our way to catch others doing something right; as we listen, bring a smile, or take the servant's towel. Love – or lack of it – will determine whether we produce angry, gang-like graffiti or flowing, symmetrical calligraphy. God help us to write well, for long after we are gone, others will be deciphering our jottings of grace – or ungrace. Will we make choices daily to be a living means of grace to others? In a sense, we could become the answer to our own prayers. An army of servant-oriented believers on the loose in the UK would surely be a myriad of living sacraments: we can become, as Thomas Merton puts it, 'a sacrament of the mysterious and infinitely selfless love that God has for (people).[1] The idea of humans choosing to be deliberate agents of grace and kindness is intriguing, and is one that has caught the attention of Hollywood.

∾ ∾

WILL WE MAKE CHOICES DAILY TO BE A LIVING MEANS OF GRACE TO OTHERS?

⌒ ⌒

Pay it forward and change the world

In this gentle, yet inspiring film, a class is challenged by their teacher to 'think of an idea to change the world and put it into action'. Young Trevor Mackinney dreams up *his* earth shaking plan – 'Pay it Forward'. The film explores the question – what might happen in the world if everyone made decisions to commit random acts of kindness towards strangers, with an expectation of nothing in return for them personally – no pay *back* – but that the person who had been shown such grace would themselves go ahead and 'pay it forward' to three other people, who in turn ... and so on. The film also inspired the launching of a 'pay it forward' web site – wwww.payitforward.com. This idea captures some-

---

[1] Thomas Merton, *No man is an island*, (Harvest books, 2002)

thing of the biblical idea of grace – those who have been forgiven freely forgive; those who have been shown compassion themselves now seek to care for others and serve them. The reciprocal nature of giving is broken in the decision to selfless generosity; but the world becomes a very much better place as the pay it forward 'virus' is caught.

Three scenes from the movie illustrate the idea. A man's car is written off in a collision, and now he has no way to get home. A complete stranger walks up to him, hands him the keys of his brand new Jaguar and insists that he takes it as a permanent gift. The recipient of the car thinks the generous stranger is demented, and hurls abuse at him – but finally takes the keys to the Jaguar.

A young boy invites a homeless person into his home so that he can take a shower and enjoy breakfast; the grateful man endeavours to repair the boy's Mum's car. And an alcoholic homeless mother is visited by her adult daughter on a rubbish dump; they sit by a blazing brazier, smoke stinging their eyes. The mother's drinking created a childhood spoiled by neglect and abuse for her daughter, but now she has come to the dump to offer forgiveness, and to invite her mother to her grandson's birthday party – on condition that she will come to the party sober.

All rather magical stuff, but is it unrealistic? Perhaps. And yet could not those of us who have heard grace news of loving our neighbours and enemies both, who have been exhorted to servant hearted service, embrace a personal choice to find ways to *pay it forward* daily? While the thought of a worldwide pay it forward movement seems unlikely to materialise, such is the grabbing nature of our humanity, isn't the world changed, not so much by huge programmes, but by a myriad of small choices? Martin Luther King was the champion and spokesman for the Civil Rights Movement in America, and as such has become the icon for the revolution that took place there: but it was Rosa Parks, a tired lady at the end of a long day, who refused to sit in the 'black section' at the back of the bus; her small, quiet protest created ripples that fuelled world change. Could we not make the world a different place by some grace choices made today? And there *is* a sense that a movement is created by those good decisions. We all create a culture around us, which is either exhortative or permissive in nature. A leader who allows their language to become lazy and begins using even mild swear words will soon notice that those around them will begin to do the same. No discussion has been had about the importance or insignificance of these things: permission has been clearly granted by lifestyle. And the same effect is true in the positive: kindness begets kindness; politeness, generosity and going the extra mile *can* be contagious. Simple acts can change the world.

It's not rocket science

Today I met, Bert, who is an angel.

Okay, Bert probably isn't an angel, unless celestial beings drive refrigerated ice cream trucks, which is always possible. And his name isn't Bert: he has a name, but I don't know it, so I christen him thus as I don't plan on forgetting him. For the sake of expediency, he shall be forever tagged in my mind as Bert. We met for thirty seconds, he did a relatively small thing, and he changed my day; perhaps my life.

It happened when Kay and I went walking in the noon blaze that is the Colorado sun. It was intended to be a brisk saunter around our neighbourhood – but we hadn't reckoned for our own geographical inadequacies (we sometimes get lost in our own house) and with the rippling, hazy heat. My forehead got a serious ultra violet bashing. In earlier years, I had a healthy head of hair that afforded some protection from the rays – in

WE ALL CREATE
A CULTURE
AROUND US

fact I sported an extended bouffant which stuck out in front of me like Florida: children and small animals would shelter in its shade. I liked my hair, comforted by the fact that if ministry ever went wrong, then I could probably get a job as a bus shelter. Now I'm so bald, people can see what I'm thinking: my naked brow was getting charbroiled.

Suddenly the ice cream truck drew up across the road from us – and two things became immediately apparent. Bert likes to sing, and sing *loud*. He was hollering a tonsil trembling rendition of some long lost Elvis song. Secondly, Bert, a white man, aspires to being a black man from the Bronx, or at least a Hollywood caricature of the same. He spoke with that delightful rap style drawl normally employed by black gentlemen in the movies. 'Hey dude, wass' happening ma man, wassup?' he enquired. Bert greeted us thus and then went on to remark that Kay and I were both looking rather flushed from the heat. We caught a glimpse of our male/female lobster faces and agreed. 'So guys', Bert continued, 'How about some nice cold ice cream – would you like some?'

Oh dear. Ice cream sounded right then like a pint of ice-cold water to a fading man lost in the Saharan dust-bowl...but we had no money with us. I stumbled with embarrassment – 'how much?' I asked Bert, a rather stupid question probably provoked by heat stroke, seeing as we had no cash at all. *Any* price was too much.

THERE ARE NEEDS AROUND ME I COULD GENUINELY MAKE A RESPONSE TO

'Nothing!' chortled delighted, benevolent Bert. 'What would you like, chocolate?' Bert jumped out of his truck, snapped open the freezer compartment and handed us an ice cream apiece. I thanked him, and then prepared myself for the inevitable sales pitch that would surely come and turn this grace act into a commercial promotion; Bert would now tell us that he could deliver these delicious lollies weekly to our home. Bert would now give us a business card, a leaflet, a speech about the greatest special limited once-in-a-lifetime offer, sign here please.

Bert did none of these things, but just said, 'Enjoy the ices – and have a nice day'. I scanned him up and down, looking for wings, halo, harp, or some other confirmation of his cherubic identity. There was none.

And as he drove away, filling his cab yet again with the yell of a tuneless melody, he left me, ice cream in hand, with a challenge. Bert had performed a random act of kindness, one that had cost him a few cents, but that nonetheless was profound. I thought of Paul's words, about how he had been 'refreshed' by the care of his friends: we of course, were complete strangers to Bert, who refreshed us. I prayed: make me a Bert.

And then I marvelled at my own fumbling response to his act of grace. It made me uncomfortable, awkward. I wanted to shout 'let me pay you' at the top of my voice, except, of course, that I couldn't. I was embarrassed by my suspicion, that there must be an ulterior motive to Bert's giving. So don't, like Mad Dogs and Englishmen, go out in the noon day sun. Be a Bert, for God's sake, and refresh someone today.

The horizon of self

Bert saw us and stopped. Obvious, yet worth noting, because I am challenged by the thought that there are needs around me that I could genuinely make a response to – yet busyness, coupled with self pre-occupation, makes me blind to them, and I rush on by, places to go, things to do, people to…see?

Marching resolutely down a church corridor some years ago, I passed a chap and offered the customary greeting in the USA: 'How are you doing?' I am embarrassed to admit that I did not stop to even wait for an answer; my question was little more than a cursory hello. I got about fifty yards farther down the hallway, when I heard a voice yell back at me from the distance, 'I'm fine, thank you…'

We surely do not see the world as it is, but through our own eyes, which much of the time are focused on survival, on the next thing, on what *we* think and feel and need. Our horizons all too often end at the point of our own needs, and we become completely unable to notice others, except in terms of what they can do for us.

The great Jewish theologian Martin Buber spoke of the distinction in our minds between treating people as *subjects* or *objects*. By objects, he meant the propensity in our world for people to see others for what use they might have for them. As we increasingly deal with inanimate objects that fulfil certain functions for us, we become ever more likely to treat people the same way. To see others as subjects is to encounter them in a way that acknowledges that they are beings at least as complex as we ourselves are. Whenever we write someone off as 'just an old coot' or a 'dumb blond' we are objectifying the person. Whenever we dismiss all young people as lazy or all non-Christians as godless, depraved pagans, we've fallen for it. When we dismiss the disabled person or the foreigner, we rule out the possibility for Christ to be revealed through a person with cerebral palsy or a Hindu … if I dismiss the people with Downs Syndrome because they have no utility for us, we limit the degree to which God can reveal grace through them. If I ignore the newcomer to my land because I can't understand his language and I have no need to relate to him, likewise I limit God's revelation to me. The more I open myself to others as *subjects*, the more I open myself to God. But Buber points out, 'we're all users if we're honest with ourselves.'[2]

And we become users when we categorise people according to what we think is their most presenting problem or challenge. Doctors who refer to patients only by their illness ('the lung cancer') are falling into a trap that is

---

[2] Michael Frost, *Seeing God in the Ordinary: a Theology of the Everyday*, (Hendrickson, 2000)

understandable because of the sheer volume of people that they see, yet is still so damaging and dehumanising. Christian leaders can look out over a Sunday morning congregation and see a crowd, rather than a familial gathering of unique individuals, each greatly loved and cared for by God. Some sadly descend to treating 'their people' as a herd, vision fodder helpfully provided for the fulfilment of someone else's dream. People become objects in our eyes when those of us who are leaders are more focused on our own dreams than on their needs. Ego can blind us to them too: so driven are we to get to the next goal, that we forget that we are pushing and shoving them up the hill of our own desperate need to accomplish. False motives make us oblivious to people.

OUR HORIZONS END AT... OUR OWN NEEDS

We saw earlier that care about the use of inclusive language is not politically correct madness: and here we must note that the way we speak of one another demonstrates that we have seen – or not seen – each other. A vicar who has disabilities shares the challenge of getting people to see past the wheelchair in which he sits:

> As a disabled person in the ordained ministry it has been interesting to see some people's response to me ... as a wheelchair user there are times when I feel the pressure to prove myself and to dispel any negative assumptions someone may have. Yet I came into the ordained ministry called by God, bringing gifts that God has given me, as a disabled person. My disability is not something I am ashamed about, but something that I hope to use in ministry.

Thankfully as the congregation gets to know me, and me them, the 'issue' of me using a wheelchair fades, to just becoming a part of me. My disability is part of who I am, and part of what God has given me to bring into ministry. I can only hope that I can be all that God wants of me.

Before we can bless, we need to see people that need blessing.

Pay it forward and mission

Last year, Michael Buerk fronted a television series, *The hand of God*, which featured one programme where a number of celebrities talked about how their faith in Jesus has affected their being in show business. Included in the line up of God-fearing luminaries was the handsome and now vintage James Fox, who dropped out of Hollywood for a number of years to become something of a street evangelist with the Navigators. The programme showed him cringing as he viewed old footage of himself out in the streets plying one of those Christian 'surveys' that used to be a popular device to help us strike up a conversation about faith.

There was no hint that Fox was denying his Christianity – on the contrary – but he was visibly disturbed by the evangelistic methods that were employed years ago; and I, for one, agree with him. I can well remember doing 'door to door work', praying that no one would be in the house and that any Alsatians lurking inside would be struck dead or at least de-fanged immediately. Nothing wrong with the door bashing, but we did do that survey thing, when actually we all knew that there was really no survey at all. Apart from quick glance at the forms in the church hall afterwards ('Ah, interesting, Mrs. Bloggs at number 47 is a Satanist...') no one was actually collating the responses – the 'survey' was just a bit of a ruse really. Not terribly ethical.

And my own attempts at evangelising the planet were terribly clumsy and forced. I didn't so much 'share my faith' as deliver a breathless monologue to any one who would listen – or not listen. Glazed eyes and much watch glancing wouldn't bother me, I'd push through regardless. And air travel was a particularly good 'opportunity', as there was no means of escape from my grinning presentations: passengers who were apparently pagan were viewed more as victims than fellow travellers.

> HAVE WE LOST SOME OF THE PLOT WHEN IT COMES TO EVANGELISM?

And it was all a bit impersonal – we talked back then about 'soul winning' forgetting, of course, that souls have bodies, stories, objections, fears and concerns. Nobody wants to be our evangelistic project at best, and a soul-scalp as worst. And, it being the seventies, when a huge fashion demon struck the earth and everyone staggered around in the most appalling clothing, we sat around in our flares and crimplene accessories and talked excitedly about conversations where we'd shared Jesus in school, the workplace – wherever we had the chance. There was culture of gossiping the gospel – and an expectation that it would have a positive effect.

But I am wondering out loud – and searching my own heart first as I do: have we lost some of the plot when it comes to evangelism? I am hugely grateful for

Alpha – much quiche has been chomped redemptively by millions around the world while exploring the great questions of life without pressure or harassment. And I am very thrilled that we discovered the poorly named 'friendship evangelism' (even if the dubious phrase sounds like a dastardly plot – 'come on, let's locate a few sinners, and give 'em the impression that we really rather like them…')

I am just a little worried that we don't hear too many people talking about time when they have actually shared their faith personally, much less actually led someone to Christ. We have just about managed to make sure that social action is viewed as being part of witness rather than being a slightly liberal cousin of it – which is wonderful – but are there people in our towns, villages and cities who think that we're quite nice and caring do-gooders – but have not got the slightest inkling that they actually need Jesus themselves? And I repeat my 'I am the chief of sinners' comment here: as part of my aforementioned aeroplane evangelism, I used to pray fervently for an opportunity to share Jesus with the person sitting next to me. I don't want to go back to that 'spot the victim' methodology, but I am sad to confess that in recent years I have been more likely to pray that the seat next to me would be empty so that I can be more comfortable. Ouch.

We've baptised around seventy people in the last couple of months in our church – and just before they take their sanctified dive under the water, most of them testify about how they came to faith. Time after time the same delightful story is told – it was a friend who demonstrated God's love, and then inked in the details by also sharing the specifics of the good news. Someone saw them, and spoke up.

Could it be that a combination of fantastic resources like *Alpha*, *Christianity Explored*, the *Y Course* and others, together with us being willing to live well and speak up for Christ, could be a potent force for the gospel? Surely a 'pay it forward' people would be far more likely to be heard. People on the receiving end of sheer kindness are prone to ask 'why?' We have an answer, which points back to the pay-it-forward cross, and the one who gave himself for us all.

WE HAVE AN ANSWER WHICH POINTS BACK TO THE PAY-IT-FOR-WARD CROSS

John Finney calls for evangelism that 'goes where people are and listens, binds together prayer and truth, celebrates the goodness and complexity of life as well as judging the sinfulness of evil, and sees truth as something to be done and experienced as well as to be intellectually believed. It walks in humility.'[3]

Are we saved? Then perhaps you – and I – should be somewhat more willing to say so. And as we do so, let's realise that we are not just delivering a message, but reaching out to people.

Grace begets grace

Two dear friends from the USA visited Britain with Kay and I last week: we prepared them for the huge culture

[3] John Finney, *Recovering the Past* (London: Darton, Longman & Todd, 1996) p.47

shock that one can feel when you cross the Atlantic. Let's face it: service – the way that people treat customers in restaurants, pub, shops – is not always that great in the lush green land that is England. We score ten out of ten for historic sites that inspire and enthral; our country lanes and villages are beautiful and unique, and our sticky pudding desserts should surely be featured on the menu for the marriage supper of the Lamb. But as for making customers feel welcomed, attended to, and appreciated, we don't always do quite so well. And so we gave our friends a lengthy lecture about being prepared for the rudeness that we Brits have all mostly got used to; it can come as quite a shock when you're familiar with walking into shops in America and being greeted by someone whose sole job is to greet you, being served a meal with a smile as well, and being told by a whole herd of grinning people that you really should have a nice day. Some Brits abroad object to all this fluffiness, of course, dismissing all the niceness as superficiality and insisting that they will have whatever kind of day they want, thank you very much indeed. But most realise that to be served graciously is a pleasant experience: personally, I'll take superficial kindness and politeness over one hundred per cent proof honest rudeness any day. And so, we prepared our friends to brave themselves for the worst.

I DECIDED TO MUG HIM WITH SOME GRACE

How disappointed we were, because they now think that we were lying. The four of us spent eight delightful days in an England which was apparently being swept by a niceness virus. Everyone we met in restaurants, garages, pubs – everywhere – was not only kind and friendly, but seemed to want to go the extra mile in helping us. We were waved at, smiled at, and bought drinks by a pub landlord who chatted with us like old friends, gave us a potted history of his delightful old pub, and even showed us the beam in the place where they hung a man because he had short-changed his tithe to the church.

What on earth was happening? Part of it, though not all, stems from the fact that our friends are themselves the epitome of grace and kindness. Even in one sticky moment, where an older lady serving sandwiches sniffed that she didn't like Americans – 'I've met some rude ones in my time', our friends smiled and tipped well and listened to her stories – and she gave them a hug and said that they were surely some of the nicest Americans she had met. And they are, as they seem to have such an ability consistently to treat people with grace, to pay it forward in that respect, and then, very often although not always, people respond in kind.

I tried this principle out when visiting my local newsagents the other day. The chap who owns the place always seems gruff, never greets his customers with any little luxuries like 'please', 'thank you', never mind 'goodbye', and not only that, he sells bread that is passed its sell-by date, surely a heinous crime. I decided to call his bluff, and mug him with some grace. Entering the shop, I called out 'Good morning…and how are you today?' He looked up, smiled, and generally acted like a very nice chap with super fresh bread. And I was chastened: while poor attitudes to service are bad for business and for life, do I wander around expecting people to be the first when it comes to offering a little sunshine and grace? Being a sacrament of blessing to others, taking the initiative in kindness not only blesses them; it can also create an unexpected culture of good will. Go ahead, make someone's day.

8

I WILL FORGIVE AS I HAVE BEEN FORGIVEN

Currently, the criminal justice system makes
no allowances for apology, which is all many victims
of crime are looking for. This alienates both
victims and perpetrators. It is refreshing to see some
public recognition of the vital role of forgiveness in
the criminal justice process.
Graham Waddington QPM of Thames Valley Police

An eye for an eye leaves the whole world blind.
Mahatma Gandhi

Chuntering

I have discovered a new word. It is 'chuntering' – and I don't know its etymological roots – it just seems to fit. *Chuntering* is something that I find myself doing more often than I'd like to admit. Perhaps you are a fellow chunterer, and we should start a support group or a club. Usually I do it alone, most often when driving.

It all starts when someone does something that has upset me; usually more than just a thoughtless word (which I can be gracious about – most of the time). It may be that someone has been consistently nasty and rude to me or about me. Levels of response get to dangerous levels when my wife or children have been hurt by these acts of unkindness. I am driving along, minding my own business, when suddenly I find myself stirred by the unfairness and the injustice of someone's actions: and so I decide that I'd like to tell them what for, loudly and clearly, with gesticulations added. The trouble is, they are not present in the car (thankfully) to be on the receiving end of my tongue bashing. But I give it both barrels anyway, yelling at them as if they were really there. So I humbly offer my dictionary definition of this word, chuntering – to rant at someone not present.

Some while ago I was engaged in an extended marathon chunter, and had pulled up and stopped at a red traffic light, while continuing to vent my spleen at my invisible passenger. Suddenly, I became aware that I was being watched, and so glanced nervously to my left. A lorry driver was watching me, eyes big and round, confused by my apparent chat with nobody in particular. The look on his face made it clear: he was of the opinion that I needed serious psychiatric assistance. My face flushed crimson with embarrassment, I decided to give him the impression that I was actually having a real conversation via a hands free telephone. I pressed an imaginary button on the dashboard to end the imaginary call on the imaginary phone. The red traffic light responded to prayer and changed to green, and I drove away, feeling very foolish indeed, and deciding to leave my rage behind me. Life felt better as I headed down the road minus my need to rant. Sometimes, however, it's not that easy.

> THE DESIRE FOR REVENGE CAN DOMINATE OUR LIVES

Love, actually

There's a bumper sticker that succinctly describes a passion for revenge: 'Don't get mad, get even.' An older inscription, expressing the same sentiment, was found scrawled as a curse in the Romans baths in Bath. The writer was obviously over-protective of his clothing accessories:

> 'Docimedes has lost two gloves. He asks that the person who has stolen them should lose his mind and his eyes...'

The desire for vengeance can certainly drive and dominate our lives. That is clear from the swashbuckling story *The Count of Monte Cristo* by Alexandre Dumas.[1] Set in early nineteenth century France, the book tells the tragic story of Dantes, a man who was wrongly imprisoned and tortured. Betrayed by his enemy Fernand, who went on to woo and marry Dantes' fiancée Mercedes, Dantes spends his every moment dreaming of freedom – and vengeance. As soon as he miraculously escapes and returns to the world with riches beyond measure, he sees it as a sign that God has opened for him the door of revenge.

But an obsession with revenge changes us beyond recognition: Dantes is not the same man who entered prison fourteen years earlier. Instead of the innocent, carefree, life-loving boy of nineteen, Dantes is now a hardened and mistrustful man in his mid-thirties. It seems a reverse baptism of sorts takes place instantly as Dantes hits the water, after being thrown off the cliff by the prison guards. He begins lying to and using those around him. He is no longer the clean-cut hero, and now, not only does he have a new name – the Count of

---

[1] Alexandre Dumas, *The Count of Monte Cristo*, (Wordsworth Classics, 1997)

Monte Cristo – but a calloused heart. The passion for revenge has ruined him for good.

Grace calls us to make hard choices about forgiving others – demanding decisions that can only come from considerable reflection, prayer and in some cases, careful counsel.

'Despite a hundred sermons on forgiveness, we do not forgive easily, nor find ourselves easily forgiven. Forgiveness, we discover, is always harder than the sermons make it out to be.'– Elizabeth O'Connor

But a deeply troubled world where so much hurt is inflicted daily – just to live on this planet means that we will all be bruised to some degree – is surely looking for what only grace can bring: the power to forgive. Many churches, homes, workplaces, friendships and marriages are being systematically destroyed every day because of a refusal to forgive, and the cycle of 'ungrace' that results.

We may be in danger of believing that forgiveness is a private matter, only applying to individuals and not relevant to the real world. But this simply isn't true. Grace could still transform the current situations in Sri Lanka, Algeria, in Sudan, in the feuding republics of the former Soviet Union. London was blown up by the IRA because of atrocities committed in 1649 which in turn were ordered by Oliver Cromwell to avenge a massacre in 1641. Crimes have continued on both sides ever since.

A recent trip to Israel demonstrated all too powerfully to me the rigidity of the circle of ungrace. I and a few others were there to see the work of Canon Andrew White of Coventry Cathedral. Andrew is labouring there to try to bring both sides of the conflict to a place of peace, and has done an amazing job so far in bringing people to the negotiating table. We met both Palestinian and Israeli leaders in what was one of the most amazing weeks of my life. On the first day, the Israelis took me to Yad Veshem, the Holocaust memorial. One cannot fail to be profoundly moved when viewing this sombre yet vivid reminder of the six million Jews who were annihilated by the Nazis, one quarter of whom were children. It is easy to understand their need to stand up for their rights and say 'Never again'. And then you meet Palestinians who are unable to work without harassment, who have lost relatives because of stray or aimed bullets fired from the young men who drive Israel's tanks, whose houses have been demolished in army raids and you realise that once again the circle of ungrace is operating: small steps towards peace and understanding are so easily destroyed by another suicide bomber or nervous, trigger happy border guard.

GRACE CALLS US TO MAKE HARD CHOICES ABOUT FORGIVING OTHERS

During the Iranian hostage crisis, the Iranians called upon President Jimmy Carter to apologise for supporting the oppressive regimes of the Shahs. He refused, stating that national honour was at stake and it was inappropriate to acknowledge past wrongs: surely a warped view of honour. The issue of forgiveness – or the lack of it – is profoundly shaping our world.

But there are good news stories from around the globe as well: in what used to be called East Germany, the parliament, in preparing for unification, made a public apology and held a moment of silence in 1990 to ask for forgiveness from Israel – after years of denying that any need for apology existed.

When Polish priest Jerzy Popieluszko was found floating in the Vistula River with his eyes gouged out and his fingernails torn off, Catholics took to the streets marching with banners that said, 'We forgive, we forgive.' In the Philippines, Benigno Aquino was due to deliver a speech in Manila – and was assassinated before he ever spoke the words, which contained a quote from Gandhi: 'The willing sacrifice of the innocent is the most powerful answer to insolent tyranny that has yet been conceived by God or man.' The Marcos regime suffered a fatal blow. In 1989 ten nations – Poland, East Germany, Hungary, Czechoslovakia, Bulgaria, Romania, Albania, Yugoslavia, Mongolia and the Soviet Union – comprising half a billion people – experienced non-violent revolutions; and in many of these, the Christian minority played a vital role.

Research published in January 2003

> shows that a significant minority of the British public – more than 1 in 5 (21%) ... think that forgiveness should form part of our judicial process, with 14% believing that if someone has been forgiven for their crime it should be reflected in their punishment. The research, commissioned by the Forgiveness Project and conducted by OMD Snapshots, also revealed that 55% of people think that forgiveness is an essential part of the healing process and 27% can imagine circumstances in which they could forgive the murderer of a close member of their family.[2]

As I write these words today, a photographic exhibition that deals exclusively with the theme of forgiveness is being held at the Oxo Tower in London. *The F Word* is a dynamic array of images by Brian Moody with interviews

---

[2] www.theforgivenessproject.com

by Marina Cantacuzino. Drawing together voices from South Africa, Romania, Ukraine, Israel, Palestine, Northern Ireland and England, *The F Word* explores and celebrates the stories of people who have survived tragedy, lived through atrocity and who have found it in themselves to reconcile or forgive. The stories are breathtaking, featuring both the well known and the 'people next door'.

One interview mentions Nelson Mandela, described as 'the epitome of forgiveness, able to reach out to all people.' While Mandela was in prison, the man who was the architect of apartheid, Hendrik Verwoerd, died. When Mandela was finally released, one of the first people he visited was Verwoerd's widow, Betsie. She received him with open arms in their house in a white suburb: surely a beautiful portrait of grace.

HOW I RESPOND
IS WITHIN MY
CONTROL

In 1999, Denise Green, an installation artist, and her husband, Bill, discovered that their son, William – who had been treated at Liverpool's Alder Hey Children's Hospital in 1992, and who later died – was one of hundreds of children whose organs were removed, without consent, for research purposes. As parents prepared for multiple burials, the Health Secretary Alan Milburn described what happened at Alder Hey as 'unforgivable.'[3]

The Greens disagreed; Denise, speaking of her choice to forgive, said: 'What happened was out of my control, but how I respond is within my control.'

---

[2] www.theforgivenessproject.com

Everyone of these stories in the exhibition – and not all end with people feeling able actually to extend forgiveness, or feeling that it is appropriate or necessary – are inspiring and authentic. One epic that is not featured there is the story of an Irishman, Billy Burns.

Billy Burns was a Bristol-based policeman who became famous in 1983 after a bank raid in the city. Trying to stop the thieves getting away with their haul of cash, he was shot by one of them. The bullet lodged in his teeth and he survived the shooting, but what made him famous wasn't that – nor was it the high-speed chase that followed before the bank raiders were caught. It was the immediate forgiveness he offered to those who very nearly killed him. 'I didn't need to think hard about it,' he comments. 'There was a natural forgiveness which I think comes from understanding your own personal position in Christ. You've got nothing to shout about, to boast about; forgiveness is the heart of the gospel and I am no more worthy of Christ's forgiveness than they are or anyone else, for that matter. What the Lord's prayer says about forgiveness should be sufficient; there's no question that we should forgive. If we don't, there's a big blockage there and there's enough in Scripture to tell us what that could cause in terms of bitterness. I have chatted to people who have gone through terrible situations, but I say you are not condoning or justifying the person's

> FORGIVENESS IS THE HEART OF THE GOSPEL

---

[4] Taken from an interview published in *The Christian Herald*.

actions, you're releasing that bitterness which otherwise will just destroy you.'[4]

Billy didn't just forgive his attackers, he was willing to meet them. Derek Rossi, one of the bank raiders, was the first to get in touch. 'He wrote to me after the trial and did apologise.' Billy's relationship with the man who actually shot him, Stephen Korsa-Acquah, has been much closer. 'He had a breakdown and went to Broadmoor prison.' From there, he asked to be able to write to Billy, and eventually not only did they correspond, but they also met up and now Stephen is going into schools in Haringey, trying to discourage other kids from a life of crime. He has asked Billy to be involved in this project – and Billy is happy to do so.

Perhaps some of us find it difficult to connect with these stories. We see Billy Burns and others like him as people worthy of our admiration, but we feel too overwhelmed by anger, or too exhausted at the thought that we might have to begin to process our pain and offer forgiveness. And it is a process. I have winced more than once in church gatherings when people have asked for ministry. A lady who has suffered the monstrous indignity of rape is told to forgive her assailant, *right now and then we'll pray for you*, and is made to feel guilty about her own entirely legitimate anger. It seems that she is being asked thoughtlessly to conjure up some instant, easy McForgiveness in a fast food spiritual drive-through. Perhaps she will also come to forgive those who, in their well meaning desire to be helpful, have added to rather than brought relief to her pain.

A woman whose brother was shot in the Northern Ireland conflict speaks of her determination but struggle on the pathway of forgiveness: 'Forgiveness is a journey. Today you can forgive and tomorrow you can feel pain all over again...' Martin Luther King once said, 'Forgiveness is not an occasional act; it is a permanent attitude.' All that said, we must begin the journey: the alternatives to forgiveness are so destructive.

The toxic power of bitterness

Philip Yancey's description[5] of the books of two Nobel Prize winning writers illustrates the power of ungrace and bitterness. *Love in the time of Cholera*, by Gabriel Garcia Marquez[6], chronicles a marriage that disintegrates over the failure of the wife to put a bar of soap out for her husband! 'Even when they were old ... they were very careful about bringing it up, for the barely healed wounds could begin to bleed again as if they were only inflicted yesterday.' *The Knot of Vipers* by François Mauriac[7] tells of another marriage breakdown, perpetuated by a husband and wife who both wait for the other to initiate grace and forgiveness – in vain. Neither one ever breaks the cycle of gracelessness, and forgives. The decision to forgive someone who has hurt us is not just for their benefit: there is a sense of self-preservation about forgiveness, as failure to forgive will produce toxic effects in our own lives,

[5] Philip Yancey, *What's so amazing about grace*, (Harper Collins, 1997)

[6] Gabriel Garcia Marquez, translated by E Grossman, *Love in the time of cholera*, (Penguin, 1989)

[7] François Mauriac, translated G Hopkins, *The knot of vipers*, (Penguin, 1985)

including an inability really to accept God's grace for our failings.

'The first person to gain from forgiveness is the person who does the forgiving and the first person injured by the refusal to forgive is the person who was wronged in the first place' – Lewis Smedes.

Archbishop Desmond Tutu was the chairman of South Africa's Truth and Reconciliation Commission (TRC). The TRC was created by Nelson Mandela's Government of National Unity in 1995 to help South Africans come to terms with their extremely troubled past. It was established to investigate the violations that took place between 1960 and 1994, to provide support and reparation to victims and their families, and to compile a full and objective record of the effects of apartheid on South African society. Tutu describes choosing to forgive as a form of self-preservation:

'To forgive is not just to be altruistic. It is the best form of self-interest. It is also a process that does not exclude hatred and anger. These emotions are all part of being human. You should never hate yourself for hating others who do terrible things: the depth of your love is shown by the extent of your anger. However, when I talk of forgiveness I mean the belief that you can come out the other side a better person. A better person than the one being consumed by anger and hatred. Remaining in that state locks you in a state of victimhood, making you almost dependent on the perpetrator. If you can find it in yourself to forgive then you are no longer chained to the perpetrator. You can move on, and you can even help the perpetrator to become a better person too.'[8]

To nurse bitterness is to place ourselves on a pathway of never-ending frustration, because, generally, whatever

---

[8] www.forgivenessproject.com

retribution actually takes place, it never satisfies our thirst for vengeance. Relatives of murdered loved ones, witnessing the execution of the killer, often express a sense of emptiness when the ultimate act of retribution is done: it is not enough to satisfy them or appease their rage.

> Vengeance is a passion to get even. It is a hot desire to give back as much pain as someone gives you. The problem with revenge is that it never gets what it wants; it never evens the score. Fairness never comes. The chain reaction set off by every act of vengeance always takes its unhindered course. It ties both the injured and the injurer to an escalator of pain. Both are stuck on the escalator as long as parity is demanded, and the escalator never stops, never lets anyone off.[9]

Our frustration is further compounded in that a continual refusal to forgive places everyone around us in the futile pursuit for perfection – a standard that we ourselves can never achieve. A sense of our own frailty and humanity is vital if we are to forgive. And bitterness poisons our relationships – the Bible says that it is a root that 'defiles many' (Heb. 12:15).

In her care for fellow Holocaust survivors, Corrie Ten Boom saw the power of ongoing bitterness tragically demonstrated. She learned that forgiveness was a daily act, and that those who had found grace to forgive their former enemies were able to return to a sense of normality again and rebuild their lives, even when their physical scars were extreme. But those who, to use her phrase,

---

[9] Lewis Smedes, quoted in Philip Yancey, *What's so amazing about grace?*, (HarperCollins, 1997)

'nursed their bitterness' remained dysfunctional. Corrie affirmed, 'It was as simple and as horrible as that.'

In *Shoah*, Claude Lanzmann's documentary on the Holocaust, a leader of the Warsaw ghetto uprising speaks of the bitterness that remains in his soul over how he and his people were treated by the Nazis. 'If you could lick my heart, it would poison you.'

What forgiveness is not

A SENSE OF OUR OWN FRALTY IS VITAL IF WE ARE TO FORGIVE

Some object to the act of forgiveness on the basis that it is unfair, in that it seems to imply that the original wrong doesn't matter – or doesn't matter very much. But forgiveness does not 'whitewash' the sin that was committed against us; on the contrary, the very act of forgiveness affirms that forgiveness is needed: it confirms the reality of the actual wrong. God does not call us to cover over evil by calling it good or neutral, but to bring grace to the reality of the hurt. Forgiveness does not mean that the natural consequences of the sin are averted – it just means that we give up our rights to be avenger in the situation.

In his book, *Total Forgiveness*[10], R.T. Kendall points out that forgiveness is not:

- Pardoning or allowing someone to escape from the consequences of a crime.

[10] R. T. Kendall, *Total Forgiveness*, (London; Hodder and Stoughton, 2001)

- Approving of or justifying what was done to us; God hates sin and calls us away from it. Forgiveness does not seek to pretend that something that was bad was really good.

- Excusing or diminishing what was done to us, or denying it in any way. Forgiveness does not try to justify what was done by looking for mitigating circumstances for someone's behaviour.

- Reconciliation – this takes two people, and may not always be possible

- Forgetting what was done – which may not be possible, as it does not erase our memories. We can decide not to dwell on them, by choosing 'not to remember.'

- Pretending that we have not been hurt

Forgiveness enables us to allow God to be God in our pain – which may involve him bringing punishment to the wrongdoer – we just surrender our need to be the judge, and we make room for the Lord.

In forgiving, we do not suspend our critical faculties. Surely one of the most misquoted and misunderstood phrases that Jesus spoke is 'Judge not that you be not judged' – as if living in a grace community means that we will never make a judgement about anything – and that any and all behaviour is to go unchecked. This is patently not what Jesus was calling for in his command that we resist *unjust* judgement. In reality, the church is called to make judgements, for example:

- About prophecy (1 Thes. 5:21)

- About teaching (1 Jn. 4:1)

- As part of loving church discipline (1 Cor. 5:13-14)

- In matters of dispute between believers (1 Cor. 6:2)

The 'judging' that we must turn from is biased, premature, hypocritical judgement that seeks to correct others whilst choosing to remain oblivious to the 'planks in our eyes', which we should deal with first (Mt. 7:3-5).

Forgiveness cannot be reduced to an emotion – in a sense it is a cold choice. Clara Barton, founder of the American Red Cross, was reminded by a friend of something especially cruel done to her many years earlier. 'Don't you remember it?' her friend asked? 'No', Clara replied, 'I distinctly remember forgetting it.' Paul Tillich says that forgiveness is 'remembering the past so that it might be forgotten'. This does not necessarily mean that the act will be erased totally from memory, but rather that we will not dwell on it, or make it the centre of our focus.

Forgiveness should never be demanded: it is a request, an appeal for grace. I was once involved in a friendship where I was repeatedly told that I had to forgive what was abusive behaviour by my (erstwhile) friend – whereupon his ranting and manipulation would start all over again. Christians have at times been told by violent or unfaithful partners that they 'have to forgive – look at what this verse in the Bible says about it.' If we seriously damage our relationships, we can squander our rights within that relationship and the abusive partner should not worsen the abuse by hurling Bible verses at their wounded spouse. Forgiveness never ever ceases to be a gift – it is for-**give**-ness.

Choosing to choose

When we forgive, we demonstrate a vital principle of grace: we become a working model that is both lovely and startling. Archbishop Desmond Tutu, in calling former South African President F.W. De Klerk to apologise for his government's actions and policies of apartheid, said that 'we should be able to teach the world, we should be able to teach the people of Bosnia, Rwanda, and Burundi ... that we are ready to forgive.' Perhaps in our small spheres, we can help make our own contribution to that lesson that is so needed in our world of strike, counter-strike, and pre-emptive strike.

Grace is available to help us hobble our way along the first faltering steps of that journey.

9

I WILL ALLOW GRACE TO CARRY ME HOME

....and grace will lead me home.
John Newton

Do you know the way to San Jose?

The flight had been long, the food abysmal and now I was squirming with discomfort in the plastic bucket seat helpfully provided by the Los Angeles airport authority. I had a three hour 'layover' (a foolish term, seeing as there was nowhere to lay, certainly not the bucket seat) before connecting with my flight to San Jose. I was excited about the few days I was going to spend with a church there, but not thrilled at all about another journey after just enduring an eleven hour transatlantic hop. I drifted into a listless half sleep, when suddenly a voice blared through the airport public address system. Its irritated tone suggested that the lady announcer was not having a happy week. Or life.

'Paging passenger Lucas!! Attention Phoenix passenger Lucas! Please go IMMEDIATELY to Gate 28a: you are delaying the flight departure, and your bags will be removed if you do not board RIGHT NOW!'

I came up out of my seat like an uncurled spring. Beside myself with panic, and imagining that the other passengers would be cheering a ritual burning of my luggage as they ejected it from the waiting plane, I gathered up my computer bag and coat and sprinted through the airport. Gasping for breath, my eyes desperately looking for a directional sign that would point me towards Gate 28a, I felt almost smothered by shame. I was holding up the entire plane. Dewy eyed grandparents would be sitting onboard weeping now, fearful that the delay would prevent them from going to see their grandchildren. Businessmen and women in designer suits would be tapping their gold pens impatiently, wondering if the multi-billion dollar deal would collapse since their plane was delayed. And it was all my fault, all because of passenger Lucas, Phoenix passenger Lucas.

> GRACE CANNOT BE FORCED UPON US

Still running, a little thought slowly emerged in my obviously tiny brain: I am not going to Phoenix. I am going to San Jose. Hooray, hallelujah and deep and lasting joy! I not therefore Phoenix passenger Lucas, I am *San Jose* passenger Lucas and I am *not* guilty of messing up anyone's life, and I can now go back and find that deliciously comfortable bucket seat and get a nap...

Take a snapshot of me, surely a Christian Mr. Bean, dashing through that crowded airport, not stopping to think clearly, but hearing my name and fearing the worst.

That's how too many of us live, hence the little book we've been sharing together. We rush through life feeling mildly bad about ourselves, sometimes irrationally guilty, sometimes hedonistically careless and sinful, and not getting it right much of the time. But I want to ask you to review with me some of those grace choices that we've looked at, and consider the challenges (and perhaps comforts) that they present. As I said in the Introduction, 'What choices is God calling you and I to make?' Choices they must be: ultimately, God offers us grace but unless we choose to hold onto it in a world and even sometimes a church which runs on ungrace, we won't benefit from it – because by its very nature grace cannot be forced upon us. It would cease to be grace if it was.

Grace will lead us...

As we make grace choices, we need to hold on to a sense of confidence and hope about the future. Grace is ours now – and will be ours tomorrow. I was speaking on marriage at a retreat recently, and suddenly felt an impulse to ask a rather unusual question. I invited everybody to close their eyes for a moment of private reflection and response and then asked: 'How many of you have a lingering feeling that, one of these days, you are going to do something disastrous that will destroy your marriage? Perhaps you feel that, while you have never had an affair now, an illicit relationship is out there somewhere, and failure is almost inevitable in your future?'

It really was a strange question – and one to which the majority of those present responded, saying that this was indeed the fearful idea that they lived with. They had been programmed to believe that disaster was almost inevitable.

Something similar was birthed in my life during my very first day as a Bible college student. One of the lecturers greeted us by telling us that within ten years, more than half of us would no longer be walking with

> ALL THE
> RESOURCES OF
> HIS GRACE ARE
> AVAILABLE TO US

God as practising Christians. We looked around the room, aghast at the thought: it was like the Last Supper as we exclaimed, 'Lord, surely not I...'

As it turns out, he was right. I weep as I bring back to mind those fresh faces of dear friends of thirty years ago: we were going to take the world for Christ. Then some of us – more than half of us – changed our minds. The reasons for those decisions are complex and are not for discussion here, but I have lived for too long with the thought that I was going to be next. Obviously, Peter serves as an example of the folly of thinking that we are beyond serious failure, as he protests that, even if every one else denies and renounces Jesus, he never will. Surely the early morning crowing of the rooster blew that false confidence apart. But I do believe that God wants us to know that all of the resources of his grace are available to us: everything that we need to navigate our way to that distant shore is at hand. As we choose to lean hard on him today, he will lead us into tomorrow, and beyond. Let's remind ourselves that all of this grace is not just about the tiny segment of time that is our life here on earth: grace calls us to look up and out to the bright future that is eternity with Christ. I fear that perhaps we have been so nervous of an otherworldly 'pie in the sky when we die' gospel, preferring to focus on what God can do for and with us in the here and now, that we have lost sight of the magnificent inheritance that grace has made ours. Sometimes I forget about heaven.

Grace will lead us home

'Can I help you?'

His voice was a little too shrill, possibly due to a too-tightly knotted tie, noose-like around a thin, scrawny throat. He smiled a professional, yet kindly smile.

'I'm here to collect a package.' He nodded. He had been expecting me.

'Mr. Lucas, isn't it?' he asked over his shoulder, striding already down the dimly lit corridor towards a back room, returning in just a few seconds, the brown box clutched in his hands. I confirmed my identity, mumbled my thanks, took the surprisingly heavy nine inch square box and headed quickly for the door.

'Sir?' I turned. What could the man want?

'Sign here, please.' I scribbled hastily, and turned to flee again.

Now I am driving through the rain, the car silent except for the droning of the windshield wipers. The car radio is silent; somehow pick-me-up soft rock doesn't seem appropriate for *this* journey. I look down at the package, sitting squarely on the front passenger seat next to me, bobbing gently up and down with the rhythm of the road. Its corners are edged with thick brown sticky tape, its smooth surface now mottled with bubbles of trapped air. No label gives a hint to its contents, just a number scrawled on one side in thick, black, felt tip pen. I flip the indicator and turn left, reach out one hand to steady my cardboard companion, concerned now lest it end up on the floor. On the straight once again, I glance again at the box, and then again, and again, a tear now trickling down my cheek, like the rivulet of rain that meanders slowly down the edge of my windscreen, a lonely escapee from the reach of the sweeping wipers. I reach out my left hand again, and lightly rest it on the cold cardboard, running a finger along the ridge of tape.

I want to hold the box, even hug it.

Just a week ago, I had been able to say that I had a father. His old smile was fading fast, and too many lines had been gouged into his face by pain's scalpel, but still, then, I was Stan's son. Now, I have only a box, and it holds all that remains of him. Beneath the wrapping sits five pounds of powdery grey ash, scooped out of a stainless steel cremator, shining, fiendish and terribly efficient. My ears cannot hear his voice, and my mind struggles to replay its sound. I used to have a dad, and now I have a box. The time for all of the funeral pomp and big black car and satin lined coffin is done; now he takes his last journey dressed down in corrugated brown.

I take the box to the old churchyard, and find the sprawling tree that had so often been his shade on distant sunny afternoons; this was his most favourite place. I am nervous, even fearful as I peel back the tape, and feel that there is some blasphemy afoot as I gaze at the naked ash, and then, courage awakened, I allow my fingers to pry deep into the powder. I empty the box on the gnarled roots of the ancient tree, enjoying how the wind lifts the grey up, up into the air. Raindrops pummel the scattered granules that find the ground, nudging them down into the soft earth.

And now, as I wander aimlessly around the gravestones, with empty box and empty heart, I notice that some ash has settled on my shoe. I leave it there, wanting somehow to take him with me always. And then, I catch sight of some faded, chiselled words formed on a gravestone one hundred and twenty three years ago. The Victorian script has survived more than a thousand rainfalls. 'Death, where is thy sting? Grave, where is thy victory?' No instant summer breaks out in my heart, but as I toss the now redundant box into a bin, and turn and walk away, head down into the rain, onward into the rest of my life, I find myself smiling, and hope peeks through the clouds.

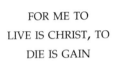

FOR ME TO LIVE IS CHRIST, TO DIE IS GAIN

Grace will be there, out of this world. Forever will be spent, not in an eternal prayer meeting, but exploring the corridors and endless portraits of God's kindness. That doesn't mean that you and I have to live each day of life hoping to expire, a perverse death wish that we are supposed to muster up if we are 'really spiritual'. I used to feel guilty for not aspiring to be hit by a truck: it almost seemed that I was not keen on rushing to heaven, which I'm not – today. Sure, Paul was able to say, 'For me to live is Christ, to die is gain' – but these are words of a weary warrior who has a sense that his time on the bloody battlefield was drawing to a close. He speaks as one who feels that his work is concluding, and that the time of transition from this world to the next is upon him. And there are many Christians who have been able to pray that prayer with Paul. Wearied by fighting sickness, homesick for heaven because a beloved husband and wife is there, they reach the stage where the aches and pains of every day are too much to bear: heaven – together with a new, pain free body – looks very inviting indeed, with the Jesus who is so full of grace waiting to welcome them there.

WE WANT TO MAKE CHOICES THAT ARE BORN OF GRATITUDE

But those of us who are praying 'heaven, here I come, but not yet, if that's okay', are still called to make grace choices in the perspective that eternity brings. We live as those who know that our existence is not mere personal survival, of no consequence or lasting significance; rather, we want to make choices that are born of gratitude, that will demonstrate grace to others, and that will therefore reverberate into eternity. And a sense of heaven will inspire and fuel us when life serves up another unwelcome dose of pain: as Jesus endured the cross, 'for the joy set before him', looking past the nails, the agony, the mocking screams, into the beyond that would be, perhaps strangely, spent with people like you and me – so we too can say, when life is horrendous, that there is yet more to come. This is truly not all that there is.

In the meantime, may you and I be people who take steps that are grace choices each day. He has chosen to be gracious: may we respond well in the decisions that we make today – and every day until it's finally home time.

Marathon grace

Earlier in this book I mentioned a vicar who is fighting cancer. His name is Simon – he is married to Nicola, and they have four sons.

Simon has always been a really energetic person, always on the go and full of enthusiasm. A couple of years ago, Simon was rapidly approaching forty, and so decided to run the London Marathon. He trained hard, ran it in 4 hours 37 minutes, and raised some £8,000 for charity in the process.

Then in January 2003 he stopped running, feeling continually under par and struggling with excessive tiredness. Blood tests were inconclusive but glandular fever was mentioned.

He went to the PCC and apologised for his lack of productivity – and yet noticed that this was a time of the greatest growth at the church that he leads; grace often flourishes in the place when human strength is low. One Monday morning he woke up with a swelling on his neck and under his armpit – which led to him having CT and MRI scans on his forty-first birthday.

He was told that there was a shadow on the left side of his lung. He needed an emergency biopsy to determine whether the problem was Hodgkin's Disease (which is treatable) or lung cancer – which is much more difficult to treat. This was the day the boys broke up from school and they were told that their Daddy wouldn't be able to play tennis, football or swim for the foreseeable future. Simon and Nicola say that they were shown such great support: people came to pray with them: a growing sense of peace was theirs.

Finally they had to return to see the consultant and get the diagnosis; Simon deliberately wore his Marathon Finishers T shirt for courage. The long wait at the hospital was agony, and finally they were told that Simon had Hodgkin's disease Stage 2. They felt somewhat elated by the news and tremendously thankful as the other alternative would have been harder to deal with. But they are realistic, knowing that they still have a battle to face. Simon will have fortnightly chemotherapy treatment for 24 weeks followed by radiotherapy, accompanied by the debilitating side-effects.

After seeing the consultant, that night they attended a large Christian meeting, Simon still wearing his marathon T shirt. Diane Louise-Jordan was speaking – and amazingly chose the idea of the marathon and the race of life as her topic. The talk seemed to be tailor made for Simon who lived and breathed the marathon for so many months. After receiving prayer, and still fully sobered by the reality of the battle to come, Nicola says, 'We left really praising God for his wonderful love and encouragement...'

Right now they are in the middle of the treatment. Nicola again:

'We feel we have entered a whole new world. But we feel truly humbled by the strength of God in our weakness and the love of those far and wide who have shown us so much kindness and support. We realize we have started the journey and there is some way to go but God willing we will get there together and God will be glorified...'

Simon and Nicola and their family are surely marathon runners, who have committed themselves to make choices based on grace, and to finish the race well. May we be like them.

And....

may the grace of our Lord Jesus Christ
And the love of God
And the fellowship of the Holy Spirit
Be with you, evermore, Amen.

If you would like details of audio and video teaching tapes by Jeff Lucas, or would like further information about any aspect if his ministry, please contact www.jefflucas.org

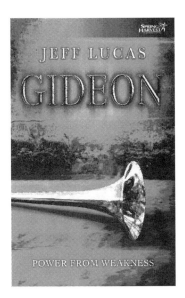

Gideon
£7.99 ISBN 1-85078-557-0

Gideon may seem like an unlikely hero but to God he was an ideal candidate for ministry. God takes weak people, meagre resources and unpromising strategies and turns them into something wonderful.

Written with humour and passion, this is an immensely readable and helpful book that will delight those who have discovered the joys of Jeff Lucas' writings before, as well as those who come to it fresh.

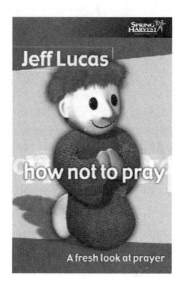

How not to Pray
£7.99 ISBN 1-85078-452-3

No one should be allowed to be so hysterically funny, insightful and transparently challenging and get away with it! You will laugh and then want to pray.
Joel Edwards, General Director, Evangelical Alliance (UK)

A liberating, humorous, down-to-earth, up-to-heaven approach, not just to the activity of prayer but how to live a prayerful, Christ-connected life.
Mark Greene, London Institute for Contemporary Christianity